REDEEMING THE HEART of CAIN

A BIBLICAL APPROACH TO MANAGING ANGER

SEAN GRAY, MA

CarePoint Ministries • Atlanta
www.ChristianCarePoint.org

CarePoint Ministries, Inc.
A non-profit faith-based ministry
www.CarePointMinistry.org
Atlanta, GA USA

CarePoint titles are available at discounts in bulk quantities. For details, contact the publisher at the above address.

Printed and Manufactured in the United States of America

Important Note: If at any time you feel you need to speak with a pastoral or professional Christian counselor, please call the church office for a referral to a member of our pastoral staff or a licensed professional Christian counselor. Church telephone number:

_____

Acknowledgements

I would like to thank the CarePoint Ministry staff and administration for their good and hard work. They have been a pleasure to work with and I applaud their vision and mission for the "Church."

Special thanks to Kelly Hawkins, a talented communicator. She wore many hats, burning the midnight oil, editing, hiring while continuing on as a full-time mom and wife.

Finally, thanks to my wife, Lora and children, Ashley and Joshua. Lora offered thoughts on anger, anger management, and healing from an intelligent, lucid, and unique woman's perspective that helped broaden the scope of this guide. Ashley and Joshua sacrificed many days and nights without their daddy so that he (I) could devote the necessary time and attention that this guide needed and deserved. My family's love, support, and sacrifice were an inspiration to me and to my approach to writing this guide.

Contents

Introduction: Overview of Anger 11

Part I: Defining Anger

Week 1: Discovering a Covenantal Heart 23

Week 2: Identifying an Angry Heart. 35

Week 3: The Anger Impact On Us & Our Relationships 49

Part II: Causes of Anger

Week 4: "Why Can't I Just Get What I Want?" 61

Week 5: Banned Anger: Cain's Destructive Heart 71

Week 6: Banner Anger: Reflecting the Heart of God. 83

Part III: Managing Anger

Week 7: Bible: Dwelling Intensely on the Heart of God 95

Week 8: Spirit: Passionately Engaging the Heart of God 109

Week 9: Bride: Living in the Heart of Redemptive Community 121

Part IV: Beyond Anger

Gospel: What it Takes to Manage Anger for Life 135

Epilogue: Supernatural Conviction: Poet's Heartache 149

References 155

Preface

A successful business man and devoted husband and father struggles with internet porn at work. In the afternoon commute he's drenched in an avalanche of guilt and shame. Later his wife asks about his day; he responds with an inane anecdote about an unruly copier and then quickly changes the subject. At a restaurant down the street, a young woman eats a great-tasting meal with good friends, and a mere 25 minutes after openly giving thanks to God for the food, she privately purges all she'd eaten in the end stall of the ladies room. A little further down the street, two men in separate cars vie for the same parking spot, and an argument and fist fight breaks out…in a crowded church parking lot. Both were to attend their first anger management class the church had sponsored, but each instead returned to his home—to mend wounds.

People struggle. Christians and non-Christians alike. We have problems, personal concerns, temptations, and issues with anger.

A Story of Anger

Recently a married couple, Reuben and Kim, told me a story of how anger nearly destroyed the relationship between them and their longtime friends, Tim and Rachel. They told me that the two couples and their families had gone on week-long retreats in the summer for years, up until a few years ago when the blessed tradition came to a screeching halt. In the Winter of the year the tradition ended, Reuben and Kim didn't think they could make the trip because of other commitments. When they told Tim and Rachel, they were disappointed but they were very understanding. As Summer approached however, Reuben discovered that it might be possible to go on the retreat but only for a shortened weekend. He told Kim and she simply called and made reservations for the weekend. She attempted to contact Tim and Rachel regarding the changes but somehow a breakdown in communication occurred. And then through busyness and forgetfulness, a significant amount of time lapsed.

Some time later Reuben was talking with Tim on the phone about sports, church, the weather, and life in general. He was unaware that, although there were attempts, Kim and Rachel had not yet made a connection about the retreat. Reuben casually brought the trip up with Tim, assuming the family excursion together was set to go. But Tim sounded surprised saying, "I thought you guys couldn't go." Now it was Reuben's turn to be surprised. When Reuben asked if Kim had called them, Tim said no. Afterwards, when Kim spoke with Rachel, Kim heard deep pain and anger in Rachel's voice as she asserted through tears, "I thought you couldn't go, and now you've made reservations without us?!" It was clear that Rachel felt hurt and wronged in some way.

The experience of feeling wronged, especially from a good friend, is a powerful and often destructive emotion. It can feel like the wrongdoer is pouring acid on the friend's heart, the powerful yet delicate part of the heart that girded the glory of love and respect in the relationship. In a moment of wrongdoing, perceived or actual, all love and respect can become dissolved and unrecognizable, leaving little but feelings of hate and anger and, possibly, a desire to part ways. Moreover, the feelings may not only seem justified, but necessary for life, necessary to go on living without ever having to trust the wrongdoer again. Dwelling in anger becomes a safe house that guards us from future experiences of overwhelming pain.

Consider the older brother to the prodigal son from the Gospel of Luke: "The older brother became angry and refused to go in [to join the party]. So his father went out and pleaded with him" (15:28). The older brother felt wronged by his dad. And in his anger he wanted to withhold relationship from all the participants in the biblical drama surrounding the perceived wrongdoing.

Anger can become a destructive storm of emotions in the lives of Christians. It is in the tempest of such strong emotions that we often, and unwisely, justify a sabbatical from our calling to be Jesus' representatives in the Ministry of Reconciliation. Anger can build walls that isolate and repel others rather than attract and unite. Yet this often seems preferable in angry moments, likely due to the fact that it offers a safe level of self-protection for our hearts and, as a result, a risk-free and a more controllable relational distance with others when we feel we have been wronged by them.

The wrongdoing doesn't have to be real in order for anger to surface. In the case of the two couples, it was clear that Reuben and Kim intended no malice towards Tim and Ra-

> The experience of feeling wronged, especially from a good friend, is a powerful and often destructive emotion...

chel. Rather, they truly wanted to be with them so that their families could experience a joy-filled, wildly adventurous, inspirational, and educational Christian retreat. Yet, through a series of circumstances the relationship was hanging in the balance.

Eventually Reuben and Kim did work things out with Tim and Rachel, at least as far as it can be to date. As it turned out there were some pre-existing relational issues between their families that weren't resolved. The issues were like smoldering embers simply waiting for the right conditions to ignite. They seem to be close again as families and as couples, but for whatever reason they have not pursued each other in any family trips or retreats since that time. Why? One possibility: a heart scoured by anger leaves scars. Scar tissue tends to be less pliable, rigid, and increasingly limited over time. For this reason, even after what seems like sufficient reconciliation and healing, the consequences of the scars may be left.

Consider the scar tissue-type consequences of anger in the relationship between the two couples and their families. For three consecutive summers they have missed out on the blessing of giving to and receiving from the retreat center. And who knows, God may have used one of the energetic and dynamic children's workers from the retreat to introduce Jesus to their children in a fresh and unique manner. The retreat center also has a very outward focus, enabling the couples to begin developing relationships with missionaries around the planet. Was there a "bigger picture" Jesus was wanting them to grasp, or a missionary in need he wanted them to support with their prayers and finances? They'll never know this side of heaven. But the bottom line, I believe, is somewhere near here: As a micro-community of two families they have simply together shared less of God in their journeys towards heaven. And it seems to hinge greatly on the destructive nature of anger. Paul says that our anger will give Satan an opportunity to establish a foothold in our lives (Ephesians 4:27).

Kim, Rachel, Reuben, and Tim wanted to establish a good tradition of summer-time spiritual unity and growth for their families. Was Satan in close proximity wanting to establish just the opposite—on-going division and spiritual atrophy? And did they give him permission to do so by ignoring what Paul said about the destructive effects of anger? What if Paul had put it this way? When you engage

> Heart Keys
> "Enemy-occupied territory—that is what this world is."
> —C. S. Lewis

in unholy anger you might as well sit down and send a masterfully written invitation for Satan to come in to your circumstances, establish residence, and wreak havoc in your life. And don't forget to send him a map and a paid subscription for a GPS tracking device so he can hound you wherever you go.

The foregoing scenario may seem a bit overly dramatic. But, in my view, it is drama based in reality. The Bible is simply very clear on the destructive nature of man's unrighteous anger and Satan's involvement. But if the Bible is as lucid as I believe it to be when it comes to this command, then (as I turn the attention on myself), why do I struggle with anger like I do? The sheer volume of anger in my life is at times overwhelming to me. Anger at work, and anger on the way to work when people are driving too slow or too fast. I get angry with my wife and my kids. I get angry with my friends and angry with my extended family. I get angry when I can't find my keys. I get angry when I plan for a day of writing and forget my research material. I even get angry with God. *Grrrr.* What's causing all this anger?

> The Bible is simply very clear on the destructive nature of man's unrighteous anger and Satan's involvement.

Introduction: Overview of Anger

"My dear brothers, take note of this: Everyone should be…slow to become angry, for man's anger does not bring about the righteous life that God desires."
—James (James 1:19-20)

If you are someone who finds it easier to read the passage above rather than live out the liberating life it offers, you're not alone. If you are someone with anger returning more quickly than you would prefer, there is hope for change. If you are someone who wants to handle anger in a godly manner—righteously and with purpose, you will find this anger management guide and support group helpful.

The term slow in the passage above means that anger should be rare and infrequent (it doesn't command, however, that we ban all anger, just man's anger). Anger should come slowly rather than quickly and not be so common that it defines an individual. In Disney's famous tale *Snow White*, the dwarfs were defined and named by specific behaviors. One dwarf in particular was named "Grumpy," likely due to the high frequency of his grumpy behavior. God becomes angered but always for the right reason; his is a righteous anger (Hosea 13:11).

In another passage of the Bible, Paul commands the Ephesians to, "Be angry…" (Ephesians 4:26, NASB). Another command then quickly follows, "…but in your anger do not sin." We should be angry for the right reason. As Christians we need to, at times, exhibit anger, yet not live a life characterized by anger.

Anger can be thought of as an archetype of the soul, that is to say, every human in all cultures experiences anger (Chapman, 17). Some individuals are good at control-

Paul commands the Ephesians to, "Be angry…" (Ephesians 4:26, NASB). Another command then quickly follows, "…but in your anger do not sin."

ling anger while others find themselves being controlled by their anger.

Both controlled as well as uncontrolled anger are a part of our lives. But since one of our goals as followers of Jesus is to reflect the holy character of God, we want to ban unrighteous anger in our behavior, and when appropriate, pursue righteous anger. But what is righteous anger? And how can it be distinguished from ungodly anger? And where does anger originate?

What's Causing All This Anger?

An innumerable amount of life circumstances can cause anger. There are two broad categories that encompass the anger we experience: interference with satisfaction and unjust assault (Allender/Longman, 55-56).

Interference with Satisfaction

First, we can become angry when we are prevented from getting what we want. Every morning I want to get to work on time but sometimes I find it difficult to fulfill my desire. And it can make me angry. One of the problems on my part is planning. In my mind I have an idea of how the morning commute should flow. I leave the house assuming there will be no road construction, no accidents, no inclement weather, nothing but the freedom to drive whatever speed I need to fulfill my desire: getting to work on time.

One morning I awoke as usual. In the pre-dawn darkness, however, I hadn't noticed that through the night the entire region had been blanketed with a fresh, cotton-like layer of snow about seven inches deep, that is, until I pressed the ice-cold button on my garage door opener. As the garage door rigidly crept upward, and with my car running readying for a quick take-off down my driveway, reality gave me a spank, the kind doctors use to bless newborns right after birth. I knew in an instant the plan to fulfill my desire was in jeopardy. After all, in order to be at work on time I needed to follow a strict adherence to 70 mph on the freeway and max out the speed limits on all the surface streets. The harsh snow, I concluded, was sure to slow me down and interfere with my desire.

It'll be tough, I thought, but since I had recently purchased a Jeep, I figured I could plow right through the deep snow. My mind continued thinking, *If I make all the lights and park in the lunch ladies parking area, which is closer to my classroom, I just might make it before the last bell rings....* Yes! I had a new plan.

First, we can become angry when we are prevented from getting what we want.

But it was short lived. I could do well on the road, sure... because I had a Jeep, but not everyone who drove that morning found sufficient traction. The traffic surrounding me on all sides, instead, moved ever-so painfully slow on this first snow of the season.

Needless to say, in the anguish of that particular morning commute, with apparent rush hour tourists—people who seemed like they had all the time in the world, who didn't seem like they had a plan or even needed a plan—I, *grrrrr*, lost my "religion." Every vehicle that wanted to merge, slow down to turn, or get in line in front of me during the endless back ups, as precious seconds ticked away, caused my heart to throb with intense anger. You may be familiar with the experience. And have you ever noticed that very few self-calming techniques seem to work?

Perhaps you've tried a similar brand of "anger management" in the car. You start off by pressing the buttons on the radio searching for a song that will calm the tempest in the cabin of your vehicle. But you instead hear annoying throat lozenge ads and tired love songs. Then you yell hoping for a cathartic release to soothe your soul. Nothing. Now your vocal cords hurt. And you're fresh out of throat lozenges. Or, in an attempt to turn a negative into a positive, you dig for the cell phone to perhaps call a good friend to fulfill the biblical directive of "daily encouraging one another." But you dynamite the thought because in the anger-filled moment you just don't feel like being constructive.

In the end there are some very valuable directions you can take when you feel anger surging through your heart. And I believe it is less about what you do in the moment of anger that helps you manage anger, because without the proper "tools" you are unarmed, unprepared, and vulnerable in the howling storm. It is rather more about what you bring to the experience of anger that is powerful and biblical, as well as helpful to managing anger. Our anger is a systemic problem based on what is going on inside our hearts rather than outside circumstances that might provoke anger.

As I reflect back on the winter-wonderland commute, I am aware that the anger came when I didn't get what I wanted. I didn't want the obstacles: the snow, the slow cars, the traffic back ups. The plan was to overcome the

Perhaps you've tried a similar brand of "anger management" in the car. You start off by pressing the buttons on the radio searching for a song that will calm the tempest in the cabin of your vehicle.

obstacles, but as it turned out, I made a plan that I could not successfully execute. I had no control over the circumstances so I felt powerless. Even owning and driving a vehicle not intimidated by snow, was at some level part of the plan. The interference with my plan unfortunately led straight to anger. But why? Anger didn't empower my car to take flight and reach my destination any sooner. What would have gotten me there sooner? Some things come to mind, to be certain. But I believe that there are larger concerns at work here. My emotions revealed something about the condition of my heart. In fact, all emotions are likely megaphones to our current mental, emotional, and spiritual internal states of being.

Anger can have purpose.

Anger can have purpose. Paul tells us to "be angry" because there are times when it is not only important to be angry but actually disobedient if we are not angry. It's the biblical component of righteous anger that, I believe, is vital to successfully managing one's anger. There are times when our anger is righteous, reflecting a quality of God, and as redeemed image bearers, we are called to reflect the character of God. Anything less would be sin, requiring repentance.

In current Christian thought, however, we generally assume we are engaging in sin only when we are angry, rather than when we are not.

In current Christian thought, however, we generally assume we are engaging in sin only when we are angry, rather than when we are not. Very few Christian preachers, for example, pound the podium with their fists with righteous anger, as Billy Graham did in the early days of his ministry. Dan Allender, Ph.D., professor at Western Seminary-Seattle, believes that Christians simply don't get angry enough. But he draws a distinction between holy (God's) anger and unholy (man's) anger (Allender/Longman, 70). Why do we often shrink from pursuing righteous anger? God, who is above the rebuke of anyone, gets angry. And we see that anger has purpose in life. The evil of Nazism, for instance, was defeated in part by the righteous anger of the American and Allied soldiers. It is hard to imagine un-angered, polite gentlemen storming a fortified beach-head, overcoming a brutal and treacherous enemy by any means necessary without an element of anger (Eldredge, 11).

My anger however during the wintry commute was not justified. It was not a righteous anger that cradled good purpose. On the contrary, I was experiencing "man's anger." The purpose of man's anger is to destroy everything in its path. Whereas God's righteous anger is designed to destroy only evil, protect what is good, and redeem hearts. Man's anger, however, doesn't have the will or desire to discriminate. That is to say, its purpose is to destroy both good and evil, anything good or bad that blocks satisfaction.

Anger doesn't have to be a life-ending attack or assault on the other person. In fact, the majority of times it is not. It can be as simple, but as equally destructive, as a shaming glance; a loud, short burst of anger (e.g., "Why did you dirty up what I just cleaned? Can't you ever…"); or a strategically placed word or phrase designed to hurt someone in a unique way. People who are closest to us can hurt us the most. This is partially due to the fact that when we are familiar with another, over time, we may detect weaknesses or vulnerabilities within him or her, and the assault may therefore occur on a deeper level because of the highly personal nature of the attack.

A man I spoke with recently said he personally struggles with a sense of low self-worth and more often than not, felt incompetent in dealing with life's responsibilities and various demands. His wife is well aware of his struggles with self-worth and is generally helpful and a source of great encouragement to him. But during our conversation he recalled how she became angry when for the second time in a year he had been passed over for a promotion. His boss detailed the primary reason: lack of self-confidence (self-worth) necessary to lead a team of line workers. His wife had been looking forward to their first-ever vacation with the monetary raise that was to accompany the promotion.

All her other friends from her women's Bible study group enjoyed vacations on a regular basis. In fact, she was the only one in her group with perfect attendance for two straight years since money was tight and she, therefore, never traveled out of town. The experience of not traveling because of a lack of money became a source of shame for her. With the promotion she had excited her hopes that a vacation might materialize. She was looking forward to sharing stories of distant lands as her friends had done countless times.

In the past she had been patient and understanding when experiencing the consequences of his low self-worth. But when she found out that he didn't get the promotion because of lack of self-confidence, she unloaded on him. One line seemed to stand out. She had used his confessed struggles against him in a moment of heated anger saying, "I can't believe how stupid you are." The first time he

Anger doesn't have to be a life-ending attack or assault on the other person. In fact, the majority of times it is not.

A man I spoke with recently said he personally struggles with a sense of low self-worth and more often than not, felt incompetent in dealing with life's responsibilities and various demands.

heard it he was stunned. At a moment of her choosing, when she became angry, she used the very words he entrusted to her to deepen the existing emotional wound and fortify his struggle.

It is moments like the account above that lead some people to conclude that it's better not to be vulnerable with anyone, because it may turn out to be too costly…too painful. Moreover, since the pain was inflicted out of an unrighteous act which is unfair and undeserved, a new anger—an anger emanating now from the victim as a result of the act of injustice may arise which, as it turns out, is the second major contributor to anger.

Injustice

Anyone with children or even a good memory of childhood is likely familiar with the emotion-filled phrase, "It's not fair!" It starts in childhood, but it never seems to go away. We simply manage to repackage and express the experience of unfair treatment. But it does not go away. *Why?* It's not because there is something wrong with us. Just the opposite, it is because there is something right with us, or perhaps better stated, there is something righteous going on inside of us. We're hardwired with the sense of justice. And the programmer of our human software is God.

Justice includes the ability to differentiate between right and wrong, good and evil, the innocent and the guilty. If, for example, a violation of innocence occurs, then an injustice has occurred. We then work to find a way to serve justice or bring justice back into the circumstance. The primary response to injustice from the followers of Jesus—those of us outside the bounds of civil government—should be to redeem the heart of the violator of justice, rather than punish the heart.

A few years ago, I was involved in the prison ministry through the church I attended. During many visits to a men's prison, I met several men who were being punished for various crimes. My goal was to demonstrate the love of Jesus, to present the message of salvation, and to simply be a good friend, whenever possible. The stories of the crimes that the men had committed were often very disturbing. And I sometimes felt anger inside after hearing their stories. At times, some of the most unnerving details would be said with a smirk or half smile. In those moments I wondered whether they were smiles resulting from nervous energy or a dark cavity of the heart. Anger within me seemed most pro-

> Anyone with children or even a good memory of childhood is likely familiar with the emotion-filled phrase, "It's not fair!" It starts in childhood, but it never seems to go away.

nounced when the smirk accompanied the details of how innocent and helpless victims were hurt, violated, or even completely destroyed. I needed God's supernatural intervention to guide my anger to be a helper/redeemer and reflect his glory rather than what seemed to come more naturally, which was to use my anger to be a destroyer and reflect more of the convict's character, or more likely, Satan's character.

The Heart of Cain

The first recorded incident in the Bible of a person mortally wounding another out of anger was Cain. Cain's anger drove him to kill his brother, a person with whom, by virtue of birth, he had a close relationship. As humans we are tempted with the same murderous-producing anger that Cain possessed. Paul writes of this clearly in 1 Corinthians when he states that the temptation individuals go through is common to everyone (10:13). Knowing that you are not alone in your struggle with anger may very well help you share with more liberty, confidence, and ease in your support group which, in turn, will prove helpful in managing your anger. And that is just the point. We benefit when we manage but not rid ourselves of anger. As believers we want the holy and powerful anger that God possesses and displays in the Bible. We no more need to abolish all anger anymore than a person on a diet needs to abolish all food. We need to possess biblical anger.

Biblical Anger

What does biblical anger look like? Anger that God heartily approves? Anger should be thought through. "In your anger do not sin; when you are on your beds, search your hearts and be silent" (Psalm 4:4). In such a situation we are neither running from our anger nor are we using it in a negative manner, rather it is spiritually productive. And it not only stops us from doing something that we will later regret, but in our anger, especially in those times when our anger beckons us to destroy with our words or actions, we learn something about the highly complex and wildly dazzling nature of God's character.

Consider how God manages his anger. In one instance God is said to be "gracious and compassionate, slow to anger and rich in love" (Psalm 145:8). The passage represents a common view of God. It's accurate, comforting, and an

What does biblical anger look like? Anger that God heartily approves? Anger should be thought through. "In your anger do not sin; when you are on your beds, search your hearts and be silent" (Psalm 4:4).

attribute that followers of Jesus should strive to attain. But God is also the one who "unleashed against them his hot anger, his wrath, indignation and hostility—a band of destroying angels" (Psalm 78:49). Those who envision God as a grandfather and angels as pudgy, adorable, pouty-faced babies may have a hard time with the passage and might therefore be tempted to dismiss it. This passage represents a rare view of God. Why is the view so rare? Isn't it also accurate, comforting, and…something we are called to be? Perhaps the part that concerns us is that we aren't called to "unleash hot anger." Or are we?

One of my best friends told me a remarkable story recently. He said that he had raised his voice in anger towards his 8-year-old daughter but then quickly proceeded to apologize to her. But she told him that he didn't need to apologize because she liked it when he became angry. My friend was surprised by her response and asked her to say more. She then went on to explain that she felt safe when she experienced his anger because, as she put it, If a bad guy ever broke into their home, he could get angry enough to defeat him and save her and her younger sisters. She felt protected as a result of his anger. But she also knows that her dad, though he becomes angry at times, is completely and unequivocally for her. She knew even at a young age that her dad had her best interest in mind which in turn made it easy for her to trust him. So his anger isn't seen so much as a threat as it is something good that preserves her soul. That is how God's anger is towards us. He uses it for our benefit. We need not be afraid of it. Although some fear does exist simply due to the sheer magnitude of his power. Similar to the experience of a U.S. jet fighter flying low at full speed at an air show. You feel an icy chill run up your spine as it thunderously roars past; the deafening sound feels like it will take over your body. But you know that the overwhelmingly powerful war plane isn't designed to harm you. Just the opposite, it is designed specifically to protect you…from an enemy.

It's the paradox of God, the same powerful anger that is used to protect is also used to destroy. But what is God out to destroy? The answer: everything that is unlike him, everything that is not completely perfect. All people have the opportunity to be redeemed, to have Jesus' perfect covering over us. Through Jesus' blood we become perfect and therefore acceptable.

It's the paradox of God, the same powerful anger that is used to protect is also used to destroy. But what is God out to destroy?

Evil exists in the world—prowling neighborhoods, workplaces, shopping centers, magazine racks, email boxes, relationships—looking for someone to destroy (1 Peter 5:8). Kindness will lead people to repentance but it will not necessarily destroy evil. The only way to rid the world of evil is to destroy it. Only God can destroy evil. In Revelation, the Devil does not receive a pardon and is not redeemed. He is destroyed. In the meantime, we benefit in eternal ways when we pray for protection from evil.

Satan asked God for permission to test Job (Job 1:6-12). God agreed and Job's world was rocked from its foundation. Job was patient at first in the middle of a very difficult trial, but after a while Job became angry with God. In his anger, Job was tempted to shake his fist at God, demanding answers. Once anger took hold, Job became a willing participant in the drama Satan schemed to drive a wedge between God and his most faithful follower. Later in the Bible there are details of another Satanic request, this time it was about Peter. Satan asked Jesus if he could have the Apostle Peter sifted like wheat (Luke 22:31). Sifting wheat involves violently separating the grain from the chaff so that it can be ground to powder, reformed, and then later consumed for the purpose of filling another. Satan was asking Jesus if he could treat Peter in a similar manner.

There are times when we might feel like calling out a band of destroying angels. I know I've been tempted to release fury. Once, for example, I was tempted to rein down fiery anger for a neighbor's 2 a.m. garage-band practice session that, even though I asked repeatedly that they respect the noise perimeter around my house, woke me out of a sound sleep…for the third time in as many nights. With every fiber of my sleep-deprived being, I felt like calling on the angels like God did in the 78th Psalm. Yet I understand that my mission and calling is more oriented towards grace and mercy rather than legalism and justice. In Colossians 4:6, Paul encourages believers to "let your conversation be always full of grace…". Why? For what purpose? So when it comes time to talk about the love and kindness of Jesus, there isn't a major disconnect between our words and our actions. If I blow my top, steam pumping from my ears while my voice fills the air with reckless words over the late-night garage concerto, for example, I am less likely to be taken seriously by unbelievers when I

There are times when we might feel like calling out a band of destroying angels. I know I've been tempted to release fury...

speak about matters of faith. What would such anger have accomplished anyway?

It might have imparted sufficient fear in the musicians so that they no longer practiced anytime after the sun sets. I would've gotten my way…enabling myself to sleep soundly, like a pouty-faced cherub. But at what price? Paul says to "be wise in the way you act toward outsiders; make the most of every opportunity" (Colossians 4:5). The cost of our anger is, at the very least, a lost opportunity to be "Jesus with skin on," so to speak…to magnify the brilliant and majestic nature of the world's only Savior.

It also was a victory for Satan who sings and squeals with unholy glee when we give in to the temptation to use our anger unrighteously. Certainly the moment of drowsy, temporary insanity can be redeemed. With prayer and the power of God, it can be redeemed with amazing and miraculous ease, in fact. But if our unrighteous anger causes a person to reject Jesus for even a single day more, then we must approach our anger not casually but with the full armor that God provides: through his Word, the Bible; through his Spirit, prayer; and through his people, followers of Jesus.

> When we drench our hearts with God's Word, encounter his Spirit on a personal level through prayer, and surround our lives with the church, followers of Jesus in a redemptive community, our very nature and essence are transformed into the image of God.

When we drench our hearts with God's Word, encounter his Spirit on a personal level through prayer, and surround our lives with the church, followers of Jesus in a redemptive community, our very nature and essence are transformed into the image of God. And our anger becomes infinitely more manageable. Choosing to walk in the Spirit rather than the flesh is difficult; a change that only God's Spirit can bring about in our lives as we continually become transformed.

As you begin this anger management guide, please read the following truth from Ecclesiastes 3:1-8.

A Time for Everything
There is a time for everything,
    and a season for every activity under heaven:
a time to be born and a time to die,
    a time to plant and a time to uproot,
a time to kill and a time to heal,
    a time to tear down and a time to build,
a time to weep and a time to laugh,
    a time to mourn and a time to dance,
a time to scatter stones and a time to gather them,
    a time to embrace and a time to refrain,
a time to search and a time to give up,
    a time to keep and a time to throw away,

a time to tear and a time to mend,
   a time to be silent and a time to speak,
a time to love and a time to hate,
   a time for war and a time for peace.

Timing is a central component of wisdom. I believe you are reading this because this is your time to work through your struggle with anger. It is your time to grow in beauty, strength, and maturity. It will get difficult, and you'll perhaps need to give up some "stuff" for a season—segments of your life that you really love doing, in order to keep you from becoming overcommitted and frustrated, and to make time for some "heart surgery" as you Redeem the Heart of Cain.

Please consider one more thought. The words are from Antoine de Saint-Exupery.

"If you want to build a ship, don't drum up people together to collect wood and don't assign them tasks and work, but rather teach them to long for the endless immensity of the sea."

And that is my hope and prayer for all of us...that rather than focusing on how to build a heart that is anger free, we would instead long for the endless immensity of God. And in the pursuit of perfect relationship with Jesus, as he increases in importance, relevance, and power, our problems, including our struggle with anger might decrease in equal proportion.

Please join me in the transforming journey throughout the following pages.

                                                    Sean

Discovering a Covenantal Heart

"You set aside all your wrath and turned from your fierce anger."

—Psalm 85:3

Welcome & Purpose

Welcome to the *Redeeming the Heart of Cain* support group for people experiencing difficulties managing their anger.

Support group purpose:

to share and discover the love, grace, and mercy of Christ Jesus with each other by sharing and bearing each other's burdens, expressing our love and care for one another, and encouraging each other so that we might gain victory over our destructive anger.

Our desire is that:

- we might experience the power and the freedom to make good choices when we experience anger;

- in our relationships, others might experience anger-free blessing; and,

- God would be glorified both in our passion to live righteously and in the new life that results from this study.

Heart Starters

"Jonathan said to David, 'Whatever you want me to do, I'll do for you...for we have sworn friendship with each other in the name of the Lord, saying, "The Lord is witness between you and me...."'"

—1 Samuel 20:4,42

"Friendship is born at that moment when one person says to another, 'What! You too? I thought I was the only one.'"
—*C.S. Lewis*

"Let's Roll!"
—*Todd Beamer, Flight 93, September 11, 2001*

Opening Prayer

Lord, thank you for bringing us together as a group to support, encourage, and help one another grow in the knowledge of you, ourselves, and each other. You are the God who gives strength to our bodies, renewal to our minds, healing in our hearts; you refresh our spirits. Help us to get to know and trust one another. We are here because we don't want anger to control our actions any longer. We recognize that this may be very difficult at times and that we cannot do this alone. We need your Word, your Spirit, and your people. Let your love, grace, and truth drench this group as we help and encourage one another in your name. Amen.

Meeting & Greeting

1

The heart of a support group is interaction! Take a moment to introduce yourself to the group. Briefly share some details of how you discovered this support group. Tell the group one "fun" fact about yourself (e.g., what is your favorite dessert/movie/song…; are you a bargain hunter, hobbyist, shower singer, runner, etc.). Feel free to write the names and some details as each member shares.

_____

_____

_____

_____

_____

Hearts of Covenant

As a group it is important that we make sure what is said or done in our group remains only in the minds and hearts of the members of our group. Trust is an important element of any relationship, and this truth is integral for our group as well. This group will be helpful only to the degree that we can effectively and dynamically interact with one another and allow God's Spirit to work in us. And for this reason, we must work to create an environment that is open, appropriately tolerant, and well-suited to effectively manage our anger.

Please read the following passage: 1 Samuel 20:42

"...we have sworn friendship with each other in the name of the Lord, saying, 'The Lord is witness between you and me.'"
—*Jonathan to David*

2 In some ways we need to have "sworn" relationships in our support group, an oath with one another to ensure trust, as friends do. Who did Jonathan and David include in their oath?

_____

_____

_____

_____

_____

3 Why do you think it was important for Jonathan and David to include the Lord in their sworn friendship?

_____

_____

_____

_____

_____

4 In your own words, how might the passage above apply to this support group?

_____

_____

_____

_____

_____

In the passage above, Jonathan and David were meeting together in a field to finalize plans necessary for the safe departure of David. It was important that the details of their meeting be kept a secret from others outside their small circle. Since David and Jonathan fully trusted one another, both knew they could openly share their thoughts and plans as well as their emotions with one another, which included weeping, tears, and kisses (20:41).

In our support group we need a level of commitment and trust similar to what Jonathan and David shared. David would have never made it out alive had it not been for the covenantal relationship he had with Jonathan. There are some people in our churches today who have not made it out "alive." Some have had their trust betrayed. They've left the church and are living their lives apart from other believers—wounded from their experience.

5 Have you had an experience with someone inside the church where your trust was at some level betrayed? If so, how did it affect your ability to genuinely trust others?

1	2	3	4	5	6	7	8	9	10
Able to Trust								Unable to Trust	

6 Looking back, what, if anything, would you change as a preventive measure to protect against a breach of trust—a covenantal pact, a more trusted friend, prayer for direction?

_____

_____

_____

_____

_____

Constructing a Covenantal Support Group

Kelly, a good counselor and former professor, recounted a time when he received a phone call from the pastor (let's call him Dave) of a client (call him Jim) that Kelly was counseling at the time. The pastor called and said, "This is pastor Dave from Jim's church. I just called to find out how Jim was doing in his counseling sessions with you." Kelly politely explained that he could not talk about the details surrounding a client. He told him that what was said in a session needed to remain confidential. The pastor went on to say that he was simply calling out of concern and wanted to know if there was anything Kelly could share about Jim so that, as Jim's pastor and spiritual mentor, he could be of help. Kelly went on to say that he could not even say whether or not he was even seeing a client named Jim. (It's simply part of an ethical oath therapists adhere to for the sake of their clients.) At this the pastor became frustrated and tried to persuade Kelly further. But Kelly refused to provide even a morsel of information. Kelly could have dropped a few hints to appease the pastor in order to relieve the conversational tension, but Kelly's priority was to look out for Jim's best interest.

7 What words would you use to describe Kelly's perspective towards Jim and their time together in counseling?

_____

_____

_____

_____

_____

8 How might our support group benefit if we adopted and reinforced such a conviction?

_____

_____

_____

_____

What are some suggestions that you can make that will cultivate an atmosphere of trust within your group? Write them down and develop a protocol; list in it action points that everyone can agree on, items that will help develop a safe and protective atmosphere in the group so that the interactions between group members can be more effective and helpful. Your group shepherd will provide you with a sample covenant that, as a group, you can do with as you will: adopt it as it is, adopt it and adapt it, or scrap it and draft your own from scratch.

9 What benefits might this support group enjoy if we built into our newly forming relationships attributes that David and Jonathan shared?

_____

_____

_____

_____

_____

Read 1 Samuel 20:17. Everything Jonathan did in the passage was keenly focused on protecting David from harm. This was clearly a well-developed relationship built on trust.

10 What, according to the passage, was the motivating factor that created such a good and unique relationship between the two men?

_____

_____

_____

_____

_____

Love is the key to creating a support group that is safe, protective, and well suited to inspire change and, in our group, manage anger.

1 Corinthians 13:7 states that "love…always protects, always trusts…is not easily angered." Satan however would want nothing more than for those in our group to toss the foregoing truths out the window and choose instead a more humanistic, defensive, and self-protective posture over our calling to love. *Why?* Meaningful change occurs when we live supernaturally. It does not, however, occur when we behave naturally, out of the flesh, which is what we do when we choose a behavioral path outside the bounds of love. Rather, living life based on our flesh rather than the Spirit is a life motivated more out of fear (fear is a tool Satan uses to moti-

vate). And while fear may work temporarily to cause behavioral shifts, it is really more like rearrangement, and therefore not at all helpful.

Heart Keys

"Love does not dominate;
it cultivates."

—Von Goethe

---

11 Can you describe a recent incident where you were easily angered? Share some thoughts about what might have provoked the anger.

_____

_____

_____

_____

_____

12 What in your view keeps you from controlling your anger on a more consistent basis?

_____

_____

_____

_____

13 How would your life be different right now if you lived a life motivated by a greater degree of love and less fear?

_____

_____

_____

_____

_____

Lucid and enduring change from the heart that starts now and carries on through eternity occurs when we live supernaturally, out of the Spirit, which is what we do when we choose to move towards others with biblical love. This is a part of the cost of following Jesus. Costly because it puts us in a position to be vulnerable, and it presents a serious potential for relational pain and turmoil. Yet enormous blessings of genuine change, heartfelt love for each other, good relationships, and liberation from anger are just some of the likely rewards that accompany such uninhibited, biblical living.

14 What in the statement above seems most attractive to you?

_____

_____

_____

_____

_____

Read 1 Corinthians 13:1-8 which describes the attributes of love.

15 Are there any parts of love in the passage that you have had a hard time living out? If so, offer details below.

_____

_____

_____

_____

16 What kind of person can you envision yourself being if you could fully live out your calling to love?

_____

_____

_____

_____

In the passage above, it states that "love is not easily angered…." The phrase may have jumped off the page when you read it. Indeed, love shines a revelatory light in darkness, exposing what we don't want, motivating us to pursue what is good, and providing an inspirational example for us to follow. True love is not easily angered; that is man's anger, unholy and unrighteous. For our purposes here let's call this type of behavior "banned" anger, because it is sin we want to ban completely from our lives. Love doesn't participate in banned anger. It would never break such a "law." When love does become angry, however, it is righteous and holy, the kind of loving anger that reflects the character of God. Let's call this type of anger "banner" anger, due to the fact that it is godly anger—worthy of banner-sized, public display. (Note: by definition banner [righteous] anger should be a rare occurrence among believers, an anger that develops slowly and without sin.)

Before we can develop the confidence that banner anger is our primary response to the world around us, we must first identify the banned anger that exists in our hearts, which we'll pursue in Week 2 of this guide.

Humor, Reflection, & Encouragement

"Never let an angry sister comb your hair!"
           —Patricia McCann

"It's the friends you can call up at 4 a.m. that matter."
           —Marlene Dietrich

"A friend is someone who knows the song in your heart and can sing it back to you when you have forgotten the words."

           —Anonymous

Adrenaline Rush

Ideas to pump your heart

Spend some time alone telling God how you feel about your anger and dealing with your anger. Ask him to speak to you about his perspective on anger, and then listen. Consider what you sense from him.

HeartMender Memory Verse

"Carry each other's burdens, and in this way you will fulfill the law of Christ." (Galatians 6:2)

Closing Prayer

Lord, thank you for bringing us together. We may not know each other very well but we are family. We have anger in our hearts yet we are made pure by your forgiveness. We are needy but we have something to offer. We are alive but we desire to be dead to our sins so that we can live for you. Help us to overcome anger so that we can live in freedom, be a blessing to others and, in doing so, hopefully, put a smile on your face. Fight this battle for us; it is too big and powerful for us to conquer. We long for your power. Our flesh is weak, but you are strong. Keep the evil one far from us through your protective hand and supreme authority. Let your love, mercy, and grace guide us as we leave this gathering. Amen.

Heartwork at Home

❶ **Read:** 1 Samuel 20:1-42. Read the *Preface* beginning on page 7 of this workbook.

❷ **Meditate:** on the value of the covenantal relationship between Jonathan and David.

❸ **Observe/Watch:** people who have good (covenantal) relationships; ask yourself: what makes it work—purpose, love, appropriate tolerance, trust, faith?

❹ **Pray:** for an openness to what God has planned for you in this study, even if it seems unconventional, feels uncomfortable, or (for a season) seems to increase your struggle with anger.

5 **Listen:** to the voices of people who support your endeavor to control your anger.

6 **Memorize:** Galatians 6:2.

Identifying an Angry Heart

"Then the Lord said to Cain, 'Why are you angry?'"
—Genesis 4:6

Heart Starters

"In the souls of the people the grapes of wrath are filling and growing heavy, growing heavy for the vintage."
—John Steinbeck

"Great discoveries and improvements invariably involve the cooperation of many minds."
—Alexander Graham Bell

Opening Prayer

Lord, thank you for bringing us back together again. You asked Cain why he was angry. And you ask us the same question. Lord, I ask that you search us and reveal the answer to us for our benefit, for the benefit of others, and for your glory. There is no greater opportunity for us than to glorify your name through our actions. Help us to discover some causes to our anger together as a group. Help grow us. Help us to trust in one another to ever-increasing levels. Lord, let truth trump in our minds and passion for you rule our hearts. Help us to give cold, refreshing water to others in your name. Drench us with your love, grace, and truth as we help and encourage one another in your name. Amen.

Heartwork at Home Review

• Share one high and one low from the week.

- Talk about your thoughts on the relationship between Jonathan and David as it relates to covenant, trust, love, etc.

- Did you have the opportunity to observe or think about a Jonathan/David-like relationship this past week? Provide some details for the group.

- Share any thoughts from the summary that you wrote.

Heart Attacked

The banned and banner anger we experience in our daily activities—construction traffic, crowded shopping mall, long lines, email, unruly copier, insensitive spouse, are lived out in various temperaments. Consider the three ways in which we respond to anger.

> ### From the Heart of Heaven
> "The heart of man is like deep water...."
> —Proverbs 20:5 NKJV

First, we can internalize our anger. When we "stuff" anger deep in our hearts it will simply surface at another point in our lives.

First, we can internalize our anger (Stanley, 171). When we "stuff" anger deep in our hearts it will simply surface at another point in our lives. Jesus in essence said that what is in our hearts will come out, usually with our words (Luke 6:45). This will likely result in any number of problems. One problem is that it greatly inhibits the ability to control or manage anger since it's much harder to monitor anger that is out of sight but ready to well up from your heart and pour out onto unsuspecting bystanders due to an unidentified "trigger."

Kirk was an all-around good guy. He was nice, generous, and somewhat quiet. In 15 years of marriage he never once became angry with his wife. And they never had an argument. He simply told himself that people in good marriages don't argue. He somehow brought himself to believe that anger was something that should not be expressed, ever. But over the years he was actually building up deep resentment and anger in his heart towards his wife and the direction of his life in general. His anger was not overt; however, he "...showed his struggle with angry emotions by withdrawing

in self-pity and engaging in critical thoughts"
(Carter/Minirth, 4).

The size of his angry heart remained a mystery until he experienced a trigger. It happened one day on a cold afternoon. He and his wife began to argue over a seemingly small incident. She became angry and, for the first time in her marriage, she yelled at him and said, "Get out of this house!" He simply looked at her for a few moments and said in an almost surprised tone, "I've been waiting a long time for you to say those very words." He turned away and left their home. Kirk later recalled the incident to me and said that all the resentment and anger he had been ignoring and internalizing had eaten away at the love he had for his wife and family. Internalizing and storing vast amounts of anger in Kirk's heart had seared it to the point that he didn't feel like anything could salvage his marriage. A short time later they were divorced. The divorce hit his four children by complete surprise.

The size of his angry heart remained a mystery until he experienced a trigger.

Read Jeremiah 17:9

1 According to the passage, what was the likely reason Kirk was unaware of his heart towards his marriage?

_____

_____

_____

_____

2 How might Kirk have benefited by expressing his anger in a safe and helpful support group?

_____

_____

_____

_____

When we internalize anger, as Kirk did, it creates a disastrous, cumulative, and sometimes relationally explosive affect. Consider the comparison to a firecracker. If you bought and then ignited one firecracker it would make a loud noise and little else. However, if you bought one firecracker each day until you collected a gross of firecrackers and then ignited them all at once, you would need an extra-long wick and good running shoes, just to escape the blast. The metaphor is an illustration to what happens when a person bottles up or internalizes anger and then releases it all at once, as Kirk did and, unfortunately in his case, with life-altering consequences.

3 Have you ever internalized or "stuffed" your anger only to have it resurface somewhere else? When the anger eventually externalized, did the anger seem more explosive because you were holding it in for so long? Offer some details.

_____

_____

_____

_____

_____

4 Did the incident that triggered your anger catch you by surprise? If so, how might you do things differently in the future to achieve a greater awareness of anger and therefore a greater ability to manage your anger?

_____

_____

_____

_____

Second, we can fully vent our anger.

Second, we can fully vent our anger (Stanley, 171). Expressing one's anger through a fully eruptive release receives more attention than internalization does. Those who fully vent their anger in the moment of their anger can be loud, intimidating, and destructive. Fully venting one's anger presents a dilemma to controlling one's anger: it often results in the venter losing some level of self-control. This brand of banned anger likely serves a purpose, however illegitimate, since such a loss of control works to intimidate others and, as well, helps release the emotional tension of anger through "blowing off steam."

5   Do you fully vent your anger in the moment of anger? If so, how do others react to you? How do you feel afterwards?

_____

_____

_____

_____

_____

Erin is a teacher who fully vents her anger. On more than one occasion I've had to leave my classroom and go to hers to calm her down. There have been times when she was yelling so loud at a student that I could hear her, even though we are a significant distance apart. There are times when she is so mad at a student she screams at him. I've seen terrified students, hoping to restrain the flow of rage, profusely apologizing to her between the angry shouts. Normally she is a great person and a fine educator. But there are those moments when she loses partial control, in the middle of a classroom, in hearing distance of hundreds of others.

Interestingly, I've never seen any other teachers go to her room during her moments of rage. They seem to know enough to keep their distance. Why? Do they think that she is angry with them? Hardly.

Most of us understand the trepidation in approaching a person who doesn't seem to have complete control over her actions. It can be frightening, motivating. Fully venting anger is useful in getting others to act according to our will. For Erin it was a way, however illegitimate, to control the behavior of disruptive students in her classroom.

> Most of us understand the trepidation in approaching a person who doesn't seem to have complete control over her actions.

6   Can you identify with either Kirk or Erin? What did their stories stir in you? Write down a few words or phrases that describe events that lead up to the experience of your anger.

_____

_____

_____

_____

_____

Heart Monitor

The following is an anger indicator checklist. Please check all that apply.

___ I have a hard time forgetting hurtful things people have said to me in the past

___ I experience anger when I'm bored

___ I become impatient when I wait in long lines, and find it hard to hide my irritation

___ I either yell or fall silent when I feel angry with someone close to me

___ I usually stay away from legitimate confrontations at work

___ When I have a problem that needs to be discussed with an individual I prefer not to go directly to that person but instead take the issue to a third party

___ I have interrupted singing praise/worship songs in my car to verbally or mentally curse another driver

___ I occasionally or frequently obsess over details/problems

___ I have been told by others that I have a bad temper

___ I have gone to bed angry even though I had the opportunity to reconcile

___ I have a hard time receiving negative feedback

___ I experience a sense of power when angry

___ I use my anger to get others to do the "right thing"

___ I have yelled at my kids

___ I don't have close friendships; I prefer to keep to myself

___ I feel more angry than sad when another person hurts my feelings

___ Following the feeling of shame, I tend to get angry (e.g., when someone laughs at me for stumbling while walking)

___ I "cut" people out of my life when I'm really angry at them

___ I tell people that I'm not angry even when I really am angry

___ I often use sarcastic humor

___ I have broken things in anger

___Nothing seems to help manage my anger

___I vent in brutal honesty when someone does something to make me angry

___I have broken objects of great monetary worth in anger

___I have hit another person in anger

___I have, with great force, punched/hit something harder than my hand

___I find ways to "pass the time," like frequently consuming too much alcohol

___I make purchases I don't need as a means of making myself feel better

___I am fearful of my own anger

___I like getting angry, it's the only time I feel truly alive

Note: If you checked five or more then this support group is the right place for you. Some anger indicators may have surprised you because they may not appear to be anger related. Yet anger can hide in the heart and take on many forms, and our response to anger can vary from person to person.

7 Using the scale below, give yourself a rating as to how well you understand what provokes most of the anger you experience—emotions, past abuse, relational heart-break, disappointments, etc.

> **1   2   3   4   5   6   7   8   9   10**
> minimal understanding   maximum understanding

Understanding is very helpful. It's not the answer to solving all our problems with anger however, but it's another useful instrument in our tool chest that helps us overcome anger, grow in maturity, and thrive as redeemed image-bearers. The psalmist offers the following insight: "How sweet are your words to my taste, sweeter than honey to my mouth! I gain understanding from your precepts; therefore I hate every wrong path. …give me understanding that I may live" (Psalm 119:103-104,144).

8 The passage states that understanding from God brings life. Put some words around what it means for you to "live."

_____

_____

_____

_____

_____

9   The Psalmist makes it clear that the source of understanding is from God rather than ourselves. Do you think this is an important distinction in the passage? If so, offer your thoughts below.

_____

_____

_____

_____

_____

10   Read Proverbs 3:5. What specifically are we called not to lean on?

_____

_____

_____

_____

_____

Heart Guard

Some Christians tend towards secular or humanistic "solutions" to our problems due to an attractive offer for a quick fix.

Some Christians tend towards secular or humanistic "solutions" to our problems due to an attractive offer for a quick fix. We lean on human understanding. But worldly understanding, rather than genuine change, can often simply lead to rearrangement of problems, destruction, or just downright ridiculous behavior. One therapist for example offered this suggestion to a client who was struggling with anger: "The next time you feel intense anger at your wife for trivial matters like unwashed clothes or an overcooked dinner try this…go out onto the front lawn and, in full view of your neighbors, stand on your head. The emotion of embarrassment will exceed the emotion of anger towards your wife which will decrease your anger towards her." Cured?

11   What lengths have you gone to in trying to overcome your anger?

_____

_____

_____

_____

_____

Heart Art

Third, we can display godly anger (Stanley, 171): banner anger! Paul provides an excellent image of the actions that should surround banner anger. "…for we are all members of one body. In your anger do not sin': Do not let the sun go down while you are still angry, and do not give the devil a foothold" (Ephesians 4:25-27). There are three relational elements to this passage.

Paul is making the point that as people we're going to be angry at some point but, (1) we shouldn't allow it to create a relational separation between ourselves and God, (2) we need to offer reconciliation before anger boils over into hate and, (3) we cannot allow an opportunity for Satan to establish control of our relationships. Truly, banner anger is an art and few of us have produced an appreciable amount of priceless works.

12 At this point do you think that through your anger Satan has already taken a foothold in some of your relationships? If so, identify the individuals by listing the names below and take some time in this moment to pray for those relationships.

_____

_____

_____

_____

_____

13 Read Ephesians 6:10-18. According to the passage (vs.11) what are you to take your stand against?

_____

Third, we can display godly anger: banner anger!

_____

_____

_____

_____

14 Part of the devil's scheme is to use your anger to secure his footing in your life. He seems to use a divide and conquer technique that often proves effective in the lives of many followers of Jesus. What does God offer us as tools to fight evil and possibly restore the relationship(s) severed and hurting from anger?

_____

_____

_____

_____

_____

Heart of Hearing

Now that we have started to lay a collective foundation of prayer to spring board off, what do the following passages suggest about a starting place for a change?

15 James 1:5

_____

_____

_____

_____

_____

From the Heart of Heaven

"...lift up a banner and proclaim it...."

—God (Jeremiah 50:2)

16 James 4:10

_____

_____

_____

_____

_____

Adrenaline Rush

Ideas to pump your heart

Take a 3x5 card, write on it "I'm feeling angry right now, but don't worry, I'm not going to attack you. But I do need your help. Is this a good time to talk?" Put this card on the refrigerator and the next time you get angry with anyone in your family, go get the card and read it to that family member.

—Dr. Gary Chapman, "Understanding and Processing Anger"

17 What are some things you can do to live out the foregoing passages in both a passionate and practical manner?

_____

_____

_____

_____

_____

Heart Break — Charting Progress

Take a few moments to gauge where your heart is right now. Consider any thoughts, views, or major life-themes that may have changed or even slightly shifted since working through this anger management guide. Write your thoughts in the inspiration organizer below.

Who I was...	Who I have become, so far...
Before this session I thought...	After this session I think...

18 What passage, quote, group interaction, or spiritual urging do you think contributed to the change or shift?

_____

_____

_____

_____

_____

Humor, Reflection, & Encouragement

"During a long life I have had to eat my own words many times, and I have found it a very nourishing diet."
— *Sir Winston Churchill*

"How much more grievous are the consequences of anger than the causes of it."
— *Marcus Aurelius*

"The will to persevere is often the difference between failure and success."

—*David Sarnoff*

HeartMender Memory Verse

"Search me, O God, and know my heart; test me and know my anxious thoughts. See if there is any offensive way in me, and lead me in the way everlasting." *(Psalm 139:23-24)*

Closing Prayer

Lord, please lighten our hearts by exposing our patterns of offensive ways of living in relating both to you and others. Give us your understanding to defeat the anger that keeps us from being what you have designed us to be. Because of you, we are greater than our circumstances. We are like the stars shining in all their brilliance when we follow your ways, namely the path of love. Lord…we desperately need you. We need you more than food, more than water, even more than the air we breathe. Please bind us together in love as a support group so that through you we can help each other. And please protect us with your power from the evil one. He doesn't want us to meet because when we do, you work in mighty ways. Help us not only identify our anger, but also your calling on our lives and your voice. Thank you for gracing us with your presence! Amen!

Heartwork at Home

1 **Read:** 1 Corinthians 13:1-7. Read the *Introduction* beginning on page 11 of this workbook.

2 **Meditate:** on the ability of love to overwhelm anger. Singing or listening to music that centers on the character of God's love and power may prove helpful.

3 **Watch:** for triggers that contribute to anger; identify them and then…pray.

4 **Pray:** for understanding, wisdom, and spiritual protection.

5 **Write:** a description of how you view yourself now. Then start to dream in vivid colors. Create a vision, with wild and bold imagination, of the kind of person you could be: fearless, faithful, beautiful, strong, redemptive, fully alive, fully reflective of God's image. Go all out if you want, scribbling hastily from the heart, with only one draft. Make it an epic mini tale with you as the hero or heroin, possessing only banner anger; with a plot, characters, good and evil, a savior, etc. (Think: C.S. Lewis' or J.R.R. Tolkien's work.) Title your work, "The Future Me." Be prepared to share part or all of your story with the group at the next gathering. Remember to keep your tale respectful, Christ-like, and fully alive.

❻ Memorize: Psalm 139:23-24.

The Anger Impact On Us & Our Relationships

"Do not be deceived, God is not mocked; for whatever a man sows, that he will also reap."

—*Galatians 6:7*

Heart Starters

"We all know people who say, 'It's the principle of the matter' to justify sustaining toxic emotions for years. As they hold onto their anger and hurt, they bleed away their energy reserves, often ending up bitter and depressed."

—*Doc Childre and Howard Martin,*
HeartMath Solution

"For every minute you are angry, you lose sixty seconds of happiness."

—*Author Unknown*

Opening Prayer

Lord, help us to not be deceived. Help us to see that what we plant we will harvest and likely eat. There is no justification for sustaining toxic emotions. Your Word tells us not to let the sun go down while we are still angry. Lord, give us the will and the power to live out your Word so that we can glorify you and encourage the body of believers, the bride for whom you died and rose from the dead by the Father's mighty power and awesome goodness. Help us to see how we hurt others and ourselves with anger. Let it inspire and drive us to align ourselves in accordance with your will to reflect your supremely unique and powerfully attractive character. Let your love, grace, and truth guide us as we help and encourage one another in your name. Amen.

Heartwork at Home Review

Briefly take turns sharing details (e.g., assigned reading, meditation, trigger identification, any answered prayers, etc.) about how God has been working in your life during the time since you last met with your support group. (Note: It is not uncommon for segments of your life to get worse before appreciable, positive movement occurs. Please, don't get discouraged! If you are experiencing an emotional decline or rise in anger frequency, don't be alarmed. It's part of the process for many at this stage in managing anger.)

Take some time to share your story, "The Future Me," with the others in your group.

1 Did writing the tale have an impact on your life—cause you to think differently? After writing your story, did anything in your life appear to decline or grow in importance?

_____

_____

_____

_____

_____

2 Out of the three, what do you think the strongest common theme in your story was: faith, hope, or love? Was there a combination of all three?

_____

_____

_____

_____

_____

Heart Attacked

As a young man, before he chose to follow Jesus, Rob was an angry person. His anger seemed most pronounced when he was out with his friends after they ran out of activities to occupy their time. One night as they were driving around passing the time on a local, city street, one of the men in Rob's car proposed a plan to buy some eggs and throw them at on-coming cars. So they scraped together some change, set out to find a convenience store and purchased a dozen extra large chicken embryos in the shell. From there they set out to create a diversion from the boredom, a form of anger (Allender, lecture notes 1993).

As the driver, Rob had little opportunity to accurately cast eggs so the three passengers deftly handled the task. Most pelted cars simply kept driving on their course, likely due in part to surprise and part desire to simply move on to a more safe location. One car, however, that was hit by one of the eggs gave chase. Rob later recalled that he and his buddies gushed: "Finally, some action!" Rob led the car on a high speed chase for a couple of miles before turning onto a resi-dential street where he ran up a curb, blew out the front tire, and came to a stop. Knowing he couldn't drive the car any longer, Rob and his friends decided to challenge the chasers, also with four passengers, to a fight. But the egged car quickly and, using good sense, wisely drove away.

Immediately, Rob and his friends went back to their car and changed the tire. Just as they were getting ready to drive away the egged car returned, with the police! The police rec-ognized that the projectile hadn't come from Rob, the driver, but from the rear passenger window. Nevertheless, the police took Rob's driver's license, wrote down the address and gave the information to the young men in the egged car. Within a month of the incident the young men who had been driving the egged car, as you might have expected, vandalized the house that was addressed on Rob's driver's license. As it turned out, however, Rob had moved several months before and never got around to updating his driver's license. Unfor-tunately, the new homeowners, innocent people, had their home vandalized by several angry young men!

> One car, however, that was hit by one of the eggs gave chase.

Heart Monitor

3 This was a real-life case study with some surprising twists. What was going on inside you as you read the foregoing account of Rob and the circumstances sur-rounding that night?

_____

_____

_____

_____

_____

4   Did the story make you angry? If so, with which person or group of people are you most angry?

_____

_____

_____

_____

_____

5   Was there anything about the story that was particularly unfair? Who in your view was treated most unfairly?

_____

_____

_____

_____

_____

6   With whom in the account above can you most identify? Why?

_____

_____

_____

_____

_____

Relate Rob's story with the Heart Starter verse which states that we harvest, bundle up, and store what we plant.

7   Can you recall an event where you planted seeds of anger only to end up harvesting, bundling, and then carrying away the anger, relationally or emotionally harboring it in a heart-shaped "storage facility"?

_____

_____

_____

_____

_____

8 What negative impact (broken objects or relationships, job loss, loss of trust, etc.) did you experience as a result of planting seeds of anger?

_____

_____

_____

_____

9 Consider your anger. Give yourself a rating as to how you view previous acts of banned anger and how they may have had a negative effect on others.

1	2	3	4	5	6	7	8	9	10

My Anger has Minimal
Effects on Others

My Anger Greatly
Affects Others

_____

_____

_____

10 Consider the anger of others. Give yourself a rating as to how you view any negative impact their anger may have had on you.

1	2	3	4	5	6	7	8	9	10

Anger of Others has
Little Effect on Me

Anger of Others
can Devastate Me

_____

_____

11 Were the two ratings different? If so, offer some possible reasons.

_____

_____

_____

_____

_____

12 Read Matthew 7:3-5. How might the passage relate to the answers in the rating scales above?

_____

_____

_____

_____

_____

13 Have you ever thought of your anger (sin) as a large piece of wood—blocking reality and the anger of others as a small speck of saw dust, a mere fragment of the wooden plank that you wield? Offer some thoughts.

_____

_____

_____

_____

14 According to the passage, what does Jesus want us to do first?

_____

_____

_____

_____

_____

_____

15 What is the result of our obedience to Jesus?

_____

_____

_____

_____

_____

_____

Heart Guard

From the Heart of Heaven

"...Satan comes and takes away the word that was sown in them."

—Jesus, Mark 4:15

One of the lies Satan uses to blur our vision is the falsehood that we are to never say no to others. Sometimes we must say no for a variety of reasons when others request that we offer our time, talent, or treasures, even when the request may have a noble purpose, as is often the case with a variety of church activities. When we feel as if we do not have the freedom to make our own decisions, anger can easily result.

One man once confided that he sold his pick-up truck so people would no longer ask him to borrow it for moving or hauling. He felt that it was wrong to say no when others needed help so he always said yes, even when he should've said no... and it made him angry. To solve the problem he simply sold the truck. But now he is struggling with guilt and shame because, even though he believes his spiritual gift is serving, he is running from his calling to serve. He's feeling angry because he feels exposed as a coward for not living by

One of the lies Satan uses to blur our vision is the falsehood that we are to never say no to others.

his conviction to serve and angry because he doesn't feel like he has the freedom to make many important decisions in life, like saying no to others.

16 What is your initial response when others demand more from you than you think you can offer? Is it usually out of a good conviction to serve or a pressure to please others?

_____

_____

_____

_____

_____

17 If your primary response is anger, is it common for you not to experience the freedom to say no? Why or why not?

_____

_____

_____

_____

_____

Heart Art

We however often live our lives as if true satisfaction will be found somewhere else.

Only God fully satisfies our hearts. We however often live our lives as if true satisfaction will be found somewhere else. Yet, when we survey our lives we find that worldly satisfaction is altogether elusive. The new carpet that once brought life to a home is now stained or worn, the new car that once generated excitement has scratches and has lost some luster, the new clothes purchased as cutting-edge fashion towards the beginning of the season at full price can already be found on the "70% Off" clearance rack. It's hard to feel satisfied in a world that doesn't fully satisfy.

18 Read Philippians 4:19. What truth is Paul communicating to the Christians in Philippi?

_____

_____

_____

_____

_____

From the Heart of Heaven

"My soul will be satisfied as with the richest of food...."

—Psalm 63:5

---

19 Are there any needs you have where you don't feel like they've been met?

_____

_____

_____

_____

20 Have unmet needs become a source of anger for you? If so, how has that anger affected others?

_____

_____

_____

_____

_____

Heart Surgery

21 Read James 5:16. What part can fellow believers play in helping you deal with your anger?

_____

_____

_____

_____

_____

22 Name a person with whom you've recently committed banned anger. According to the passage, what can prayer help achieve in your relationship with that person?

_____

_____

_____

_____

_____

Adrenaline Rush

Ideas to pump your heart

Listen to the hurt, anger, and rebuke of others who have been negatively affected by your anger.

Humor, Reflection, & Encouragement

"Be nice to your kids. They'll choose your nursing home."
—*Marcus Tullius Cicero*

"Anger is a killing thing: it kills the man who angers, for each rage leaves him less than he had been before—it takes something from him."

—*Louis L'Armour*

"I don't have to attend every argument I'm invited to."
—*Author Unknown*

HeartMender Memory Verse

"A fool gives full vent to his anger, but a wise man keeps himself under control." (Proverbs 29:11)

Closing Prayer

Lord, our hearts are engaged in this anger guide because we want to rid our lives of anger and live for you. We see that anger gets in the way and hinders your call on our lives to love others as ourselves. Help us to see how the seeds of anger we plant become weeds in our lives that choke out the healthy plants and the flowers. Please keep Satan far from us so our thoughts can remain focused on you. Bless our efforts to pursue your heart instead of a heart that reflects the nature of Cain. Thank you for gracing us with your presence! Amen!

Homework

❶ **Read:** Galatians 6:7-10.

❷ **Meditate:** on the consequences of planting from the sinful nature vs. the benefits of planting to please the Spirit.

❸ **Observe:** the look on people's faces whenever they are on the receiving end of your banned anger.

❹ **Pray:** that God would guard your heart, tame your anger, and reconcile any relationships broken from anger.

❺ **Write:** a love letter to those you have hurt with banned anger. Include in it an apology; acknowledge any harm that may have been done and communicate a desire to reconcile. Carry the love letter in your pocket for at least a week as a helpful reminder, then discard; or offer the love letter to the affected individual.

❻ **Memorize:** Proverbs 29:11.

❼ **Do:** Week 4 in preparation for next week's group.

"Why Can't I Just Get What I Want?"

"You want something but you don't get it."
                                        —James 4:2

Heart Starters

"If your desires be endless, your cares and fears will be so too."
                                        —Thomas Fuller

"If any of you lacks … he should ask God, who gives generously to all without finding fault, and it will be given to him."
                                        —James 1:5

Opening Prayer

Lord, thank you for bringing us back together again. Help us with the tension that exists between legitimate, holy desire and a demanding spirit that leads to anger and other destructive tendencies. Lord, give us hearts that are full of gratitude and awe, with an attitude that says, "My needs are met, I can rest." Please turn the problems and struggles we have into relational pathways towards you and others. You are a great God and it is our privilege to be here in your presence in a unique and special way. Let your love, grace, and truth guide us as we help and encourage one another in your name. Amen.

Heartwork at Home Review

- Share some details about the love letter that you wrote.

- Was it a difficult task or were you able to write it with relative ease?

- In what ways was it helpful in dealing with the anger you felt towards the person for whom the letter was written?

- Did you keep the letter or give it to the person?

- If you offered it to the person what was the outcome?

(Note: Share only the details you are comfortable sharing and believe to be appropriate. The goal of our interaction is to be helpful and encouraging. Follow your heart.)

Heart Attacked

I'll never forget the look on Kate's face as she told me how she had 15 job interviews only to be turned down every time. She followed up on every one of them, and each time she learned that she was either in the running for the position or, more often it seemed, the runner-up. Ever since she was a little girl her only desire was to teach. She worked hard in college to get straight "A's," she leaped on every opportunity to volunteer in after school programs, taught at summer camps, joined every relevant professional organization, went through the wild rigors of substitute teaching, stacking her resume with every attractive element.

And as a Christian she prayed. Her main prayer before every interview? "Lord, you know my heart and my passion, and the effort that I have put into my pursuit of being a teacher. I would very much like the teaching position for which I am about to apply. But, Lord, my highest prayer is this: Let your will be done."

1 What is your "highest" prayer when praying for something you desire with all your might?

_____

_____

_____

_____

> I'll never forget the look on Kate's face as she told me how she had 15 job interviews only to be turned down every time.

Heart Keys

But, Lord, my highest prayer is this: Let your will be done.

After the prayer, especially after the last sentence, "Let your will be done", she felt peaceful and even confident. The interviews, she recalled, generally went very well. But an unusual circumstance always seemed to pull the position just out of her reach. One experience was especially difficult. She went to the interview. It went well and they offered her the job. Excited, thankful, and full of praise to God, she went to the restaurant job where she had been working as a part-time waitress and submitted her two week notice.

She went home later that night and played her voice mail. It was the principal that had hired her earlier in the day. The principal spoke the following words on the recording, "Don't quit your job. We've just been told by the administration that there isn't enough money for your position. We can no longer offer you the job. Good luck with your plans, however. You're an excellent candidate; you shouldn't have any problem finding the job of your dreams." He had no idea she was living in a nightmare.

2 Think about Kate's life-long efforts. If you were sitting down with her over coffee hearing her story for the first time, what advice would you give to her?

_____

_____

_____

_____

_____

3 What role did she allow God to play in her life?

_____

_____

_____

_____

_____

4   If you were Kate, with whom would you be most angry?

     __ The principal, for offering and then pulling the job offer
     __ Yourself, for not waiting longer to quit the previous job
     __ God, for knowing and seemingly keeping you from your fondest desire

---

Heart Monitor

5   Use the scale below to identify the level of anger you experience when something interferes with satisfaction or desire.

    1   2   3   4   5   6   7   8   9   10
    Not Very Angry   Very Angry

_____

_____

_____

6   Use the scale below to identify the level of anger you experienced 5 years ago when something interfered with satisfaction or desire.

    1   2   3   4   5   6   7   8   9   10
    Not Very Angry   Very Angry

_____

_____

_____

7   Was there a change? Did your rating show an increase or a decline in the amount of anger you experience when you don't get what you really desire? If there was a change either way, write down your thoughts as to what may have contributed to the movement—loss, betrayal, sickness, marriage, children, new job, friend, support group, prayer, etc.

_____

_____

_____

_____

_____

Heart Guard

Read Psalm 33:20.

8 What does this passage tell us about the value of waiting?

_____

_____

_____

_____

9 What does the Lord provide us with when we wait on him?

_____

_____

_____

_____

Read Ephesians 6:16.

10 What does Paul exhort us to do with the shield in the above passage? What can using the shield accomplish?

_____

_____

_____

_____

_____

11 Satan attacks us in our weak areas. What in your view are your "weak" areas—where, when, or how do you most often experience an attack from Satan's arrows?

_____

_____

_____

_____

_____

12 We may or may not carry around a shield. For this reason the passage may seem a bit difficult to put into practical use on a daily basis. But read the passage again. What is the shield comprised of?

_____

_____

_____

_____

_____

Heart Art

Read Romans 10:17.

13 According to the passage, where does faith come from?

_____

_____

_____

_____

_____

14 In your own words, how does the foregoing passage possibly speak to the value or importance of scripture memorization?

_____

_____

_____

_____

_____

Heart Surgery

After playing the voice mail from the principal, Kate simply sat stunned in her chair. A flood of emotions swept over her during that time. She felt shame, anger, conflicted, hopeless, and a sense of futility. She then got up and flew into a rage, screaming, throwing objects, shaking her fist at God. Afterward, she slumped into her bed and cried until exhaustion ushered in sleep.

> She then got up and flew into a rage, screaming, throwing objects, shaking her fist at God.

From the Heart of Heaven

"My heart is in anguish within me.... 'Oh, that I had the wings of a dove! I would fly away and be at rest...far from the tempest and storm.'"

—Psalm 55:48

15 In a matter of a few moments Kate had gone from envisioning herself in a rewarding, well-paying profession that would likely span 30 years to wondering if her boss at the restaurant would let her go back to waiting tables. Do you think she was justified in her anger? Why or why not?

_____

_____

_____

_____

16 What other emotional responses in addition to anger might Kate have displayed?

_____

_____

_____

_____

_____

To be blocked from gaining what we want forces us to wait, and we despise the helplessness of waiting because it stops us from moving toward satisfaction. Waiting intensifies pain because it forces us to see that we are dependent creatures (Allender/Longman, 56).

17 Can you think of a time recently where waiting (at a grocery store, in traffic, at a bank) created a significant level of anger?

_____

_____

_____

_____

_____

18 At what point did the anger subside? And what caused the anger to subside—time, prayer, help from a friend, venting, internalization, not sure?

_____

_____

_____

_____

_____

Read Proverbs 16:9. Fill in the blank.

19 "In his heart a man _____ his _____ but the Lord _____ his _____."

(Word Bank: course, steps, determines, plans)

20 Regardless of what causes your anger to subside, what does the verse above tell us about who is ultimately in charge of our efforts to alter, say, our anger?

_____

_____

_____

_____

_____

Humor, Reflection, & Encouragement

"People who fly into a rage always make a bad landing."

—*Will Rogers*

"Blessed is he who expects no gratitude, for he shall not be disappointed."

—*W.C. Bennett*

"May he give you the desire of your heart and make all your plans succeed."

—*King David, Psalm 20:4*

Adrenaline Rush

Ideas to pump your heart

Listen to what your heart wants opposed to what you've been conditioned to want.

HeartMender Memory Verse

"The Lord is my shepherd, I shall not be in want. He makes me lie down in green pastures, he leads me beside quiet waters, he restores my soul.." (Psalm 23:1-3)

Closing Prayer

Lord, thank you for our time together. We know that desire is a good thing, something you placed inside us. Help us not to demand that our desires be met. Help us not to get angry when we don't get our way or when something blocks us from pursuing something we want. Lord, we pray that you would consume the small and petty things that seem so big yet in the larger frame of life are really nothing at all. Lord, please grow large in our field of view. Block out all the stuff that holds us back from reflecting your awesome nature and character. Help us to be like you in our anger. Help us to desire what you desire and reject the things you reject. Protect us. Thank you for gracing us with your presence! Amen!

Heartwork at Home

❶ **Read:** Romans 10:1.

❷ **Meditate:** on the "bigger picture" of Paul's heart's desire.

❸ **Observe/Watch:** for the "flaming arrows" of Satan.

❹ **Pray:** the "closing prayer" from above every day this week.

❺ **Write:** down three things due to waiting or a blocked desire which contribute to banned anger. Contact a trusted friend or support group member who will help you manage the anger through advice, accountability, and prayer.

❻ **Memorize:** Psalm 23:1-3.

❼ **Do:** Week 5 in preparation for next week's group.

Banned Anger: Cain's Destructive Heart

"...they attack me without cause."
— *King David, Psalm 109:3*

Heart Starters

"Deserves it! I daresay he does. Many that live deserve death. And some that die deserve life. Can you give it to them? Then do not be too eager to deal out death in judgment. For even the very wise cannot see all ends."
— *J.R.R. Tolkien*

"Why do the nations rage...? The kings of the earth prepare for battle...against the Lord and against his anointed one. 'Let us break their chains,' they cry, 'and free ourselves from this slavery.'"
— *Psalm 2:1-3, NLT*

Opening Prayer

Lord, thank you once again for bringing us together. Lord, on our journey, help us gain the freedom and strength to overcome the moments in our lives when we've been unjustly treated. Sometimes our hearts scream for revenge in the trials of fierce injustice. Help us not to be too eager to deal out words of anger and death in judgment. Help us, together as a support group, to encourage and strengthen one another to accomplish our goal of reflecting your character above our own. Let your light shine in our dark emotions so that we may glorify you, overcome our anger, and be a beacon that lights a path to you for us and those who want to know you. Let your love, grace, and truth guide us as we help and encourage one another in your name. Amen.

Heartwork at Home Review

Write down in one sentence the importance of something you've seen, heard, or read as it relates to banned anger. Focus on how the group work and homework made you think and feel. Take turns reading your sentences. Provide encouraging and/or helpful feedback to others when appropriate.

_____

_____

_____

_____

_____

Heart Attacked

> Jimmy sat stunned as he heard the words from his angry and crying mother echoing down the hall into his bedroom, "We're divorced, kids! You hear that? We're divorced!"

Jimmy sat stunned as he heard the words from his angry and crying mother echoing down the hall into his bedroom, "We're divorced, kids! You hear that? We're divorced!" His parents had gotten a divorce over the Winter but didn't tell their four children until Spring. Young Jimmy was devastated. All the legal wrangling, custody issues, living arrangements had been sorted out in court, but the lives of the family on the surface to friends, neighbors, and co-workers and even to the children, remained unchanged. In an angry moment, however, during an explosive argument with Jim's dad, Jim's mom belted out the life-wounding words above. Jimmy's life was forever changed. It was the Spring of 1994. He was 12-years-old.

1 Why do you think the mother blurted out the life-altering news in such a harsh manner as opposed to sitting down with her kids to carefully and lovingly explain why their lives would be going on without their father?

_____

_____

_____

_____

_____

After some of the shock wore off Jim began to cry. His sisters were too young to know what was going on. They simply sensed trouble. Neither one of Jim's parents ever came to comfort or speak with him about the news of the divorce that night. Their anger had apparently overwhelmed any compassion. Jim cried alone until sleep brought the desired effect: a numbness to his young soul.

The following day Jim went to school feeling devastated. The bus ride, the endless walk through the halls, the slamming of steel lockers, the ringing of the early bell all seemed like surreal sounds produced by a dream. Sleep was no option in class, but neither was class work. He simply sat at his desk thinking the same thought over and over, *This is not fair! This is not fair! How can they do this to me?* Feeling helpless and unfairly treated he gradually moved toward anger. With each angry thought he gained a greater sense of power and an increased sense of control over the situation. For the first time since hearing the devastating news, interestingly, Jimmy began to feel...better.

The following day Jim went to school feeling devastated.

2 Do you detect any "red flags" in the behavior of the people cited in this case study? If so, what do you observe?

_____

_____

_____

_____

_____

3 What is the "fuel" that is beginning to ignite Jim's anger?

_____

_____

_____

_____

_____

4   Is there any part of this section that you can relate to—the unfair treatment, sense of control or power through anger?

_____

_____

_____

_____

_____

> **Over the years Jim moved from being a victim of anger to an agent of anger.**

Over the years Jim moved from being a victim of anger to an agent of anger. He discovered that while he couldn't use his anger to bring his parents back together again, he could use his anger to sometimes "motivate" people to do the things he wanted them to do, things that he thought were, according to his standards, fair and just. Others didn't view his anger as a mere motivational tool but rather a means of intimidation and control. And on occasion people would kindly confront Jim's anger. Jim would simply dismiss their admonitions as a misunderstanding or a weakness on their behalf. Jim however was simply making excuses, and very few friends.

5   Victimization and agency tend to be very separate issues in our culture. How would you respond to the phrase, "We are all victims and we are all agents of sin"?

_____

_____

_____

_____

6   Do you view yourself as both a victim of sin and an agent? Which do you tend to focus your attention on?

_____

_____

_____

_____

7 Can you think of a time when you used your anger to get another person to do what you wanted them to do? Provide some details.

_____

_____

_____

_____

_____

Heart Monitor

Jim developed a personality of anger that can be traced to a specific event. He had a heart-crushing experience, he found a heart-numbing salve and, to cope, nourished an anger-shaped heart. Do you have a time in your life where you can pin-point an event that triggered anger that you have carried from that moment until this day?

Your Heart-Crushing Event

_____

(Example: Jim's parents' divorce)

led to commitment to…

Discovery of Heart-Numbing Salve

_____

(Jim felt better when angry)

What your life looks like now…

How Anger Has Shaped Your Life

_____

(Jim's life marked by intimidation and isolation)

Paul exhorts us to "Sing and make music in our hearts to the Lord, always giving thanks…" (Ephesians 5:19).

8 How often would you say you sing to and make music to and for Jesus in your heart?

_____

_____

_____

_____

_____

9   Are you always giving thanks—why or why not?

_____

_____

_____

_____

_____

10   What do you think will happen to the shape of your heart if, to a greater degree, you sing and make music for Jesus and continually give thanks to him?

_____

_____

_____

_____

_____

Heart Guard

> "When I was a child, I talked like a child, I thought like a child. When I became a man, I put childish ways behind me" (1 Corinthians 13:11).

> **When we were children we moved in self-preserving ways for survival as a way to cope with a broken heart.**

When we were children we moved in self-preserving ways for survival as a way to cope with a broken heart. Now that we are grown we don't need to use the same tactics; we don't need the same preservatives for our heart.

11   In what ways might you still use the tactics of a child to protect your heart from relational pain?

_____

_____

_____

_____

_____

_____

> "Do not be like Cain, who belonged to the evil one and murdered his brother. And why did he murder him? Because his own actions were evil and his brother's were righteous."
>
> —1 John 3:12

12 Looking back, has a fellow believer come to you in a heart of love and righteous concern against your anger but you reacted negatively towards that person out of a commitment you may have made to yourself never to feel the same child-like pain again? Offer some details below.

_____

_____

_____

_____

_____

13 Has there been a shift over time, for better or worse, in the way you respond to a righteous rebuke by a concerned fellow believer? If so, what do you think has contributed to the change in your behavior?
If worse, might it be because of increased anger-producing elements in your life, including stress, financial trouble, family/health problems?
If better, might it be because of accountability, increased Bible reading, turning to God and prayer, less stress, better relational systems of support?

_____

_____

_____

_____

_____

Heart Art

"Above all else, guard your heart."

—Proverbs 4:23

There are many tragic segments to Jim's story, but one glaring point stands out: There was no one who was willing or able to help young Jimmy guard his heart.

There are many tragic segments to Jim's story, but one glaring point stands out: There was no one who was willing or able to help young Jimmy guard his heart. No one ever spoke tenderly to his heart in an attempt to mend the relationally shattered pieces. Just the opposite occurred, the divorce announcement was like a knife in Jim's heart. But the manner in which it was communicated was like the same knife twisting with malicious force. Following the relational knifing and emotional torture, Jim was left alone to figure out a way to stop the bleeding from the wound that was created by the people he trusted most.

14 How might his life have been different if the divorce itself were handled differently?

_____

_____

_____

_____

_____

15 How might your life be different now had someone demonstrated a greater interest in guarding your heart when you were younger?

_____

_____

_____

_____

_____

Create-a-Scene

Express ideas/thoughts/emotions from the answer above in pictorial form below. (Key: Create/draw from your heart; don't rationalize your feelings as you draw.)

Create-A-Scene Pictorial Box of Healing and Inspiration

Heart Surgery

Our goal in this anger management guide is to redeem the anger in our hearts, the heart of Cain. We no longer want to be filled with the same anger and be associated with the evil one as Cain was, which he lived out in a dramatic manner by killing his own brother.

The Following verses can help us redeem the heart of Cain that, sometimes—uncontrollably and even destructively—throbs in our chests.

Our goal in this anger management guide is to redeem the anger in our hearts, the heart of Cain.

16 Read Acts 16:37-40. How did Paul respond to unjust treatment—did he ignore or acknowledge the issue of unjust treatment and fairness—did the act of injustice control Paul or did he control his anger towards injustice?

_____

_____

_____

_____

_____

17 Paul loved the Corinthians first and continued to love them even when they neglected to love him back. Read 1 John 4:19. Why do you think Paul was able to love so well? As it relates to anger, how might you apply the passage to your life?

_____

_____

_____

_____

_____

Adrenaline Rush

Ideas to pump your heart

Watch the movie, *Monster-In-Law* (2005). Focus on the elements of anger from the movie that are similarly present in the first four weeks of this anger management guide.

Humor, Reflection, & Encouragement

"Expecting the world to treat you fairly because you are a good person is a little like expecting the bull not to attack you because you're a vegetarian."

—Dennis Wholey

"Unrighteous anger…draws our deepest desires to the surface and leaves us emptier than we were before."

—Dan Allender

"If thou suffer injustice, console thyself; the true unhappiness is in doing it."

—Democritus

HeartMender Memory Verse

"If we confess our sins, he is faithful and just and will forgive us our sins and purify us from all unrighteousness." (1 John 1:9)

Closing Prayer

Lord, thank you for our time together. We know that life is unfair and we cannot let such circumstances control our behavior. Help us not to ignore unfairness but to move towards it in love, the kind of love that can only come from you as a supernatural gift. Help us to use this gift of love not to live angrily but to give generously. We no longer want to have in our chests a heart which beats to the rhythm of Cain. Let our hearts beat like yours and love powerfully in the process. Protect us from the evil one who tells us that we cannot wait for your justice. We can wait and by your intervention we will wait for your perfect timing and justice. Thank you for gracing us with your presence! Amen!

Homework

❶ Read: the book of 1 John.

❷ Meditate: on the manner in which God cleanses us and our hearts.

❸ Pray: for God to protect your heart when a wrongdoing or unjust assault occurs.

❹ Listen: to the tone of desperation that leads to anger in the Mother-in-law from the movie, *Monster-In-Law*.

❺ Memorize: 1 John 1:9.

Banner Anger: Reflecting the Heart of God

> *"He (Jesus) looked around at them in anger and, deeply distressed at their stubborn hearts, said to the man, 'Stretch out your hand.' He stretched it out and his hand was completely restored."*
>
> —Mark 3:5

Heart Starters

> *"The world needs anger. The world often continues to allow evil…it isn't angry enough."*
>
> —Bede Jarrett

> *"Anyone can become angry. That is easy. But to be angry with the right person, to the right degree, at the right time, for the right purpose and in the right way—that is not easy."*
>
> —Aristotle

Opening Prayer

Lord, thank you for bringing us together again. Please help us with this sometimes controversial topic. Help us to display your anger, anger that is righteous, good, and purposeful…anger that is worthy of a banner with your name splashed across it with holy pride and defiance of the evil that is in the world. Help us not to confuse the purpose of anger: to restore the hearts of your children and destroy evil. Let your love, grace, and truth guide us as we help and encourage one another in your name. Amen.

Heartwork at Home Review

Discuss the movie, *Monster-In-Law*. Reflect on the elements in the movie that focused on the anger that was present due to desires that were blocked, what the anger motivated the characters to do, and how the exposure of the anger led to redemption and ultimately, reconciliation.

_____

_____

_____

_____

_____

_____

Heart Attacked

I was caught off guard when Sue told me, through a hollow-tone filled with fear, of the violation she experienced just a week prior in my classroom. *How could I have not seen what was happening right in front of me?* I didn't know it right then, but the actions of righteous anger in my heart would be needed in the days following our conversation.

Sue, a shy and quiet student, had just told me that a boy who sat behind her in my classroom had been touching her in sexually inappropriate and humiliating ways. She then apparently went home and told her mother. Her mother then sent her to tell me about what was occurring. She then told me that she was afraid to tell me about the boy's malicious actions, saying she feared that she may have done something wrong to provoke the boy to violate her. I was surprised by her disturbing admission.

My first response was to assure her that she did absolutely nothing wrong. I told her as plainly as I could that she did not deserve such dreadful treatment. I told her that she should never again be apprehensive about protecting herself from a bully or an abuser. She seemed relieved and slightly more relaxed following our conversation. It was just over a month into the new school year. She was 14-years-old.

> I didn't know it right then, but the actions of righteous anger in my heart would be needed in the days following our conversation.

1 You may be sensing some anger in your heart right now. If so, do you view it as banner anger that should be encouraged or anger that should be repented of and banned?

1	2	3	4	5	6	7	8	9	10

Ban the anger   Unfurl the banner of anger

_____

_____

_____

2 Where on the scale did you place yourself? Why?

_____

_____

_____

_____

3 Did you detect any peculiar details about the story? What stood out to you?

_____

_____

_____

_____

4 What would you have done next?

_____

_____

_____

_____

My next step was to report the incident to administrative authorities and then verify the story with her mother. Throughout the week a comprehensive picture of the problem began to emerge. This wasn't the boy's first offense. Within the confines of the new school year he had also been in altercations with two boys. Both were special needs students. Sue was quiet, shy…innocent. It could be said that each of the three victims were, in general, "weaker" than the perpetrator. A picture began to emerge for me: the boy in question was preying on the weaker students in the classroom. Each incident had a similar theme. He found weak students, sexually or physically violated them, and then cleverly intimidated them into staying silent to protect his behavior. A cold chill fell on me as reality came into full view: I had an actual predator in my class.

The administration called the police, but they contended that since both were minors nothing could be done. The administration called me and said that the boy would be suspended for a couple of days. I was surprised by what I considered to be a lenient consequence for such a serious offense. I told the administrator that I had some thoughts I needed to share. I sat down with her and explained my concerns about the boy's predator-like tendencies, citing evidence to back my conviction. The administrator agreed with my assessment but confessed that her hands were tied, that there was no other place to put him. Within three days the boy came back to the room and, with a smile on his face, arrogantly sat down in his original seat, right where the abuse had initially been perpetrated...right behind Sue.

> I was surprised by what I considered to be a lenient consequence for such a serious offense.

5 How might have banner anger energized or motivated the administration to seek an alternative to their plan and position?

_____

_____

_____

_____

_____

Heart Monitor

Many times through the foregoing ordeal my heart pounded with intense anger. And my anger worked to motivate me to righteous action. I displayed my anger both to the administration as well as the young perpetrator. How can I know for certain that I possessed banner anger rather than anger that should have been banned? My greatest desire was to speak up for and to protect the innocent students from the wrongdoer.

6 Read Proverbs 31:8-9. Fill in the blanks below.

"Speak up for those who cannot speak for themselves, for the rights of all who are destitute. _____ up and _____ fairly; _____ the rights of the poor and needy."

(Word Bank: defend, judge, Speak)

7 How does the anger that is present in the passage above differ from banned anger from the last chapter?

_____

_____

_____

_____

_____

8 What, if any, apprehension do you have in using anger to motivate you to action, even if it is a truly righteous cause?

_____

_____

_____

_____

_____

Heart Guard

God says to be angry but warns against crossing the line into sin. Anger tends to come naturally for us, but we battle the urges continually. This week's group on the other hand is designed to encourage and even celebrate anger. Satan wants you to be angry but in the exact opposite manner that God has designed. Satan finds both pleasure in your anger and trembles in great fear because of it. Is it any wonder there is such a great tension and disagreement on the matter?

> God says to be angry but warns against crossing the line into sin.

9 Why do you think Satan would find pleasure in much of your anger? Which type of anger might it be?

_____

_____

_____

_____

_____

10 Why might Satan tremble at an expression of your anger? Which type of anger would cause Satan to tremble with fear?

_____

_____

_____

_____

_____

Heart Art

Read Hebrews 3:7-19.

11 What kind of heart does the writer of Hebrews warn against having? (vs.12)

_____

_____

_____

_____

12 With whom was God angry for forty years? (vs.17)

_____

_____

_____

_____

_____

13 What oath did God declare in his anger? (vs.11,18)

_____

_____

_____

_____

_____

God becomes angry. And in his anger he destroys sin. Read Genesis 1:27.

14 As you consider the verse above, do you think as image-bearers we should reflect the side of God that becomes angry? Why or why not?

_____

_____

_____

_____

_____

Heart Surgery

When the boy with the predatorial tendencies sat down in his old seat behind Sue, energized by righteous anger, I moved into a mode that fully desired to protect Sue's heart, as well as the perpetrator's heart and, at the same time, destroy sin. I went to the boy and sternly said, "Get up out of the chair!" As you might imagine he asked "Why?" (People who abuse others tend to portray themselves as unsuspecting and unaware. It helps them carry the persona of innocence which is key to perpetrating abusive behavior because, if caught, others are more apt to view the perpetrators as victims rather than agents of abuse.)

In the intense interaction with the boy I wanted him to know beyond any doubt that I was ablaze with anger. Yet in my anger I didn't yell, demean, or intimidate. Rather, in that moment, the anger I experienced was complete power and a holy desire to destroy. I did not fear losing control nor did I fear the power I experienced. My anger had nothing to do

In the intense interaction with the boy I wanted him to know beyond any doubt that I was ablaze with anger. Yet in my anger I didn't yell, demean, or intimidate.

with frustration, it wasn't about a desire that was blocked (Week 2); and I wasn't yelling internally, "Not fair!" (Week 3). Rather, as far as I can determine, I merely reflected the part of God that is angry for the purpose of protecting the good while destroying the bad.

> ### Heart Keys
> ...the anger I experienced was complete power and holy desire to destroy. I didn't fear losing control nor did I fear the power I felt.

Sue observed my anger and felt safe again.

Sue observed my anger and felt safe again. She understood that someone was looking out for her best interests. Soon afterwards, Sue began to thrive in my class and the positive change in her self-worth and self-confidence was obvious. Shortly after the incident she sketched a portrait of me and offered it as a gift, out of gratitude I assumed. A year after she left my class she came back again, where she offered a verbal thanks for my intervention. The boy was expelled shortly after the incident. I can only hope and pray that his experience in my classroom exposed any fallacy he had about getting away with hurting others and not expecting negative consequences, for his benefit and for the benefit of others throughout his life.

15 What are your thoughts on the way I handled the situation? with Sue? with the boy?

_____

_____

_____

_____

_____

16 Can you recall a time in your life where you followed the Lord's leading and acted out of banner anger to destroy sin, to protect someone's heart, or both? Share some of the details in your group. Resist any urge to hold back on some of the good things you may have accomplished due to the redemptive nature of your anger. Use this time to encourage others with an account of anger that is reflective of God's character.

_____

_____

_____

_____

_____

Heart Break — Charting Progress

Take a few moments to gauge where your heart is right now. Consider any thoughts, views, or major life-themes that may have changed or even slightly shifted since working through this anger management guide. Write your thoughts in the inspiration organizer below.

Who I was...	Who I have become, so far...
Before this session I thought...	After this session I think...

17 What passage, quote, group interaction, spiritual urging, do you think contributed to the change or shift—how might your interactions with God and others be different as a result of the change?

_____

_____

_____

_____

_____

Humor, Reflection, & Encouragement

"I know the world isn't fair, but why isn't it ever unfair in my favor?"

—Edmund Burke

"Thou shalt not be a victim. Thou shalt not be a perpetrator. Above all, thou shalt not be a bystander."

—Holocaust Museum, Washington, DC

"God designed and blessed anger in order to energize our passion to destroy sin."

—Dan Allender

HeartMender Memory Verse

"Be angry and yet do not sin...." (Ephesians 4:26, NASB)

Adrenaline Rush

Ideas to pump your heart

Meditate on the three aspects of our call to "speak up," "judge fairly," and "defend the rights of the poor and needy."

Closing Prayer

Lord, thank you for this study of your Word and the views of those who believe in you. Help us to recognize your truth, and give us the will to change our views when they don't match with yours. Give us the wisdom to handle banner anger. Lord, just as we don't want to give up camping because fires are dangerous, help us not to give up on our call to anger simply because it can be dangerous. Help us rather to live our lives more in tune with your heart through your Word, your Spirit, and your people. Please keep Satan far from our hearts. Thank you for gracing us with your presence! Amen!

Homework

❶ Read: Proverbs 31:8-9.

❷ Observe/Watch: for ways to live out the foregoing three aspects of Proverbs 31.

❸ Pray: for wisdom in discerning banned and banner anger.

❹ Listen: to God for the answers to the prayer above through God's Word (The Bible), God's Spirit (prayer) and his people (fellow Christians).

❺ Write: a summary of your thoughts. List some things that you still want to know about the topic and then brainstorm ways to find the information. Take some time researching and then describe what you discovered.

❻ Memorize: Ephesians 4:26.

Bible: Dwelling Intensely on the Heart of God

"Blessed is the man who...meditates on your word day and night."

—Psalm 1:1-2

Heart Starters

"If you do not wish to be prone to anger, do not feed the habit, give it nothing which may tend to its increase."
—Epictetus

"May my lips overflow with praise...may my tongue sing of your word...."
—Psalm 119:171-172

Opening Prayer

Lord, thank you for bringing us together again. We want to know what's on your heart. We want to dive into the deep waters of your Word so that we see in every direction the crystalline liquid of truth. We want our actions, including our anger, to glorify you. We cannot do this alone. Help us not to feed the habit of anger but to starve it. Help us to focus on you day and night so that we might become more like you. Help us to do this together for your glory. Let your love, grace, and truth guide us as we help and encourage one another in your name. Amen.

Heartwork at Home Review

- Talk about any thoughts you had or actions you took on Proverbs 31 to speak up, judge fairly, and defend the rights of others in need.

- Discuss some of your thoughts on banner anger. Did you discover anything in your research regarding banner anger that you thought might be helpful for the group? If so, share some of the data you discovered.

_____

_____

_____

_____

_____

Heart Break

1 What do you feel you most need to manage your anger right now? Why?

__ This anger management guide

__ Working through self-help type steps to overcome anger

__ Trying harder to love rather than be angry

__ Anger therapy such as a punching bag, counting, or counseling

Heart Attacked

In writing this guide I have been tempted to offer "quick fix" solutions to problems of anger that have, for some, taken decades to foster and intensify.

In writing this guide I have been tempted to offer "quick fix" solutions to problems of anger that have, for some, taken decades to foster and intensify. I have also felt the pressure to list steps to overcoming anger because that is how most anger management books are written and presented. And I do offer some suggestions that I think may be helpful. But the bottom line is this: when you complete this guide, you will still struggle with sin because you are on this side of heaven, still looking through a dark glass, rather than face-to-face, as 1 Corinthians 13:12 states. The danger in approaching any material written by people in hopes that it will "cure" you is three-fold.

First, unless you are called Home after reading this sentence, you will continue to struggle with anger after you complete the material (hopefully to a lesser degree while, at the same time, moving in a direction to overcome anger). Second, because you continue to struggle with the issue, there is a strong temptation to give up, throw your arms up, and simply give in to the anger. Third, if steps are offered as a "fix" to anger and you still feel angry at the end of the process you will feel like the promise was broken, your heart-felt hopes and high expectations will be dashed, and a whole new problem may ignite: a heart of cynicism. This is lived out in an attitude that says, Why bother reading a book or going to a support group or wasting money on counseling? It doesn't "work" anyway!

2 Do you have any experiences with "quick fix" solutions? In what ways did you or didn't you find them helpful?

_____

_____

_____

_____

_____

A friend of mine recalled an incident where he completed a book designed to help him with some of his personal struggles. He said that when he finished the book he threw it across the room and yelled, "This doesn't work! This book is a bunch of bull!"

3 My friend was looking to the book as a cure for his sin and struggles. How might his attitude have been different had he approached the book as a helpful resource to aid him in his journey towards heaven rather than as a cure for sin and struggle?

_____

_____

_____

_____

_____

The purpose of the anger guide is to help you gain one or two transformational steps further from your struggle and, equally, become closer to the heart of the Father. Life changes seem to be comprised of a few dramatic changes and an innumerable amount of small shifts that lead us to a particular place in life. Both have brought all of us to this very moment in time. And when we obey the will of God the changes in our lives, both small and large can lead us towards God and away from anger.

4 Read Romans 12:2, how can we know the will of God?

_____

_____

_____

_____

Focusing on the impure, untrue, ignoble, and so on can have catastrophic effects.

I believe the well-known phrase, "what an individual puts into one's body is what comes out" has a ring of truth to it. Focus on something with intense interest for a significant period of time and it will shape your thoughts and deeds. Perhaps it is why Paul tells the Philippians to dwell on the elements of life that are "pure, true, noble, lovely, excellent, praiseworthy;" an so on (4:8). He understands that focusing on such things can cause a believer to be transformed for the good—spiritually, mentally, emotionally, and physically. He also understands that the opposite is true as well. Focusing on the impure, untrue, ignoble, and so on can have catastrophic effects.

5 How do you think what you've invested/spent your time dwelling on in the past has shaped your thoughts and beliefs as a person and a Christian—is your current thought life reflective of what Paul said we should dwell on?

_____

_____

_____

_____

> ### *Heart Keys*
> Focus on something with intense interest for a significant period of time and it will shape your thoughts and deeds.

In the movie *Lord of the Rings*, one of the characters, who had dual personalities, was named both Golem and Smeagol. He was a highly conflicted character; his speech was labored and he primarily crawled on all fours. He wasn't human, or so it seemed. He appeared to be in a state of constant desperation and obsessive neediness. Mostly he was hyper-dependent, and he had a hyper-singular focus on one thing and one thing only: the ring. Why? As the story goes, he found a ring that was made from an evil entity. Those who took possession of the ring were tempted, beyond what they could bear, to engage in evil behavior. For hundreds of years Golem did little else but dwell on the ring, staring at it day and night, stroking it, speaking tenderly to it. As it turned out, Smigley was actually a human before he discovered the ring. Dwelling on the ring had not only altered his mind; it had also caused him to lose everything and everyone in his life (like severe addictions often do). The intense interest and unending focus on the ring had actually absorbed his former bio-physical nature, transforming him into an entirely different creature.

6 If you watched the movie *Lord of the Rings*, what do you remember feeling about Golem? Even if you didn't see the film, to what extent can you identify with his character-conflicted nature, hopeless desire, willingness to do anything to connect with an addiction, a sense that you aren't the same person you used to be?

_____

_____

_____

_____

_____

7 During the course of your day how does what you dwell on affect your behaviors and the way you attempt to address the issue you listed above?

_____

_____

_____

_____

_____

Heart Monitor

At any moment, we are all being transformed, either in the pattern that takes us towards God or towards this world...

At any moment, we are all being transformed, either in the pattern that takes us towards God or towards this world—a world that often says, "Be self-absorbed. Find your ring and stare at it, stroke it, invest all your time with it, speak tenderly to it." For some, this is a house; for others, a career; for many, a relationship, or the dream of something better. Often they are good things. But when blessings from God become idols, which is anything we place above God, even good things can become a ring-like focus which can shape our thinking and set the course for who we are becoming. We tend to not realize the depth of the idolization until the entity is taken away. We find out what we are dependent on when we lose a job or career, when we are rejected by a friend, or when a dream is shattered like glass which can, among other detrimental aspects, end up being an anger-producing nightmare. I believe God wants so much more for us.

8 If you can identify idols in your life, what would happen if you set aside your idol(s) and began dwelling on and trusting in God's sovereignty and provision?

_____

_____

_____

_____

_____

9 Differentiate between serving God and dwelling on God. Give some examples.

_____

_____

_____

_____

_____

10 On the whole, and in your view, what do you think God wants us to dwell on in the same way Golem dwelt on the ring? Try to be specific.

_____

_____

_____

_____

11 Read Romans 12:1-2. What will happen when we are transformed by the renewing of our minds—how can this passage help you in differentiating between banner anger and banned anger?

_____

_____

_____

_____

We are transformed, in part, by the written Word in the Bible. The Psalmist wrote that he meditated on God's Word all day long. And he was blessed and chosen by God to have his writings become part of God's eternal Word: The Bible. Jesus meditated on God's Word and he used it to fight Satan and resist temptation, helping him emerge from 40 days in the wilderness with the only available option in God's design: Total victory over sin and Satan.

> Jesus meditated on God's Word and he used it to fight Satan and resist temptation...

Heart Guard

"…Satan comes and takes away the word [of God] that was sown in them." (Mark 4:15)

12 What affect would the preceding passage have on your ability to dwell on God?

_____

_____

_____

_____

_____

13 In the box below, take a moment to write a prayer to combat the actions of Satan that were described to us by Jesus in Mark 4:15.

Prayer of power and love to destroy evil box

Heart Surgery

My son has a friend named John who has seen the movie *Star Wars III* several times. He has the complete set on DVD. He can recite what seems like hundreds of phrases from the series. He recites them throughout the day, whenever something reminds him of one of the movie scenes, which seem to continuously overflow from his conversational interactions. I've heard him humming the theme song casually or when at play. He has Star Wars posters, toys, weapons, clothes, and more. His mind, body, and heart are clearly immersed in the fantasy.

14 What is the inevitable result of dwelling intensely on something other than God? How is it reflected in John's life?

_____

_____

_____

_____

_____

15 Read Luke 6:43-45. Consider how intensely dwelling on something for an extended period of time allows it to become stored in our hearts.

_____

_____

_____

_____

_____

16 How might your struggle with anger be mitigated if you begin to shift what you dwell on so that you can store a greater amount of "good" things in your heart?

_____

_____

_____

_____

_____

Use the charts below to begin shifting what enters and overflows from your heart.

Think of an incident or event recently where you stored anger in your heart; where the anger overflowed; and describe the impact of the experience on others and/or yourself.

Stored Anger	Overflow Anger	Fruit/Effects of Anger
List specific anger	List specific words/deeds	List details of results

Name one or two anger-producing issues or perhaps a negative theme that you want to stop dwelling on. Then name one or two elements in your life you want to begin dwelling on.

Stop dwelling on:

Heart storage chamber

Creates storage space to...
Begin dwelling on:

Heart storage chamber

Heart Break

17 How angry would you say you were when you first arrived for this group today?

1   2   3   4   5   6   7   8   9   10
Not Very Angry   Very Angry

_____

_____

_____

18 How angry would you say you are now compared to the level of anger at the onset of today's group?

1   2   3   4   5   6   7   8   9   10
Not Very Angry   Very Angry

_____

_____

_____

19 Take note of the two scales, did you record a reduction in your level of anger ? If so, describe in general what you engaged in during this study which might have contributed to altering your feelings of anger.

_____

_____

_____

20 What are two things you can do to begin focusing on God and God's word with greater interest and intensity?

_____

_____

_____

_____

_____

Humor, Reflection, & Encouragement

"I am saying pornography hurts anyone who reads it, garbage in, garbage out."

—*Jerry Falwell*

"The strongest influences in my life...are always whomever I love. Whomever I love and am with most of the time, or whomever I remember most vividly. I think that's true of everyone, don't you?"

—*Tennessee Williams*

"For where your treasure is, there your heart will be also."

—*Luke 12:34*

Adrenaline Rush

Ideas to pump your heart

Observe nature and people; try to catch glimpses of God's "invisible qualities, eternal power, and divine nature."

HeartMender Memory Verse

"Do not conform any longer to the pattern of this world, but be transformed by the renewing of your mind. Then you will be able to test and approve what God's will is—his good, pleasing and perfect will." (Romans 12:2)

Closing Prayer

Lord, thank you for bringing us together again. You are faithful. Help us in our journey towards you and away from the patterns of this world. Renew our minds so that, in addition to so many other negative elements in the world, our anger will daily become less and less of a factor in and over our lives and in our relationships. Help us to immerse ourselves in your Word, meditating on it day and night. Help us to dwell in unity with you, resting in your sovereignty and provision in our lives. Let your Word and your presence glitter in our hearts like expensive and precious diamonds. Let the overflow from our hearts be like fragments of eternity for you and others. Let it make our words a priceless gift to you. Please keep Satan from taking your Word from us. Thank you for gracing us with your presence! Amen!

Homework

❶ Read: Psalm 1:1-5; 19:1-14; 119:48; Romans 1:20.

❷ Meditate: on the passages above and the wonder of his creation.

❸ Pray: the Song of Moses and Miriam, Exodus 15:1-13.

❹ Listen: to Bible passages about God's character set to music. Check online or at your local Christian bookstore.

❺ Write: a list brainstorming all the ways you might de-emphasize thoughts that dwell on "patterns" of this world and a list that emphasizes new ways you can emphasize thoughts that dwell on renewing your mind and storing up "good" things in your heart.

❻ Memorize: Romans 12:2.

Spirit: Passionately Engaging the Heart of God

"And pray in the Spirit on all occasions with all kinds of prayers and requests."

—*Ephesians 6:18*

Heart Starters

"The deepest desire of our hearts is for union with God. God created us for union with himself: This is the original purpose of our lives."

—*Brennan Manning*

"Would you like to pray?"

—*Lora Gray*

Opening Prayer

Lord, thank you for bringing us back together again. Help us to live a life that is marked by focused, intense, and continual prayer. Give us a passion to connect with you; to trust and enjoy you. Transform our lives and overcome our strongholds by which the evil one holds us captive. Help us to be the Bride who is interested in readying herself for you and your holy pleasure. Let your love, grace, and truth guide us as we help and encourage one another in your name. Amen.

Heartwork at Home Review

Share with the group parts of the list from Week 7 that were most helpful in de-emphasizing thoughts that dwelt on the patterns of this world and describe which ways were most helpful in emphasizing new ways to dwell on renewing your mind.

_____

_____

_____

_____

Heart Monitor

1 Which phrase below best describes your prayer life as it relates to anger?

___ Lord, take away my anger

___ Lord, make me a nicer/better person

___ Lord, keep me from my sin

___ Lord, teach me to reflect your character

Consider the foregoing phrases: "take away…", "make me…", "keep me from…", and "teach me." Notice two elements contained within. First, all are good prayers. No question. Yet, secondly, only one can ignite a prayer life in a way the others simply cannot. Our prayer life should include all of the above prayers but rather than having our prayer life marked by telling God what he should add and subtract in our lives, our prayer life should be marked by an openness of "teach me" more of what God might want to offer in our one-on-one time with him.

> Our prayer life should be marked by an openness of "teach me" more of what God might want to offer in our one-on-one time with him.

2 Read Romans 8:26-27. As it relates to your struggle with anger, what best describes your thoughts/feelings after reading this passage?

___ Futility; why bother praying if I don't know what to pray for?

___ Hopeful; he knows more about prayer than I do

___ Relieved; I can give my burdens over to him

Constructing a Heart of Prayer

God communicates to us uniquely through three different means: his Word, the Bible; his Spirit, prayer; his people, the church.

3 What has been your experience in hearing God "speak" when you pray—I sometimes feel led to action when I pray; I hear thoughts but no words; I can "see" Bible verses in my head; my prayers seem to bounce off the ceiling; I pray and then I do?

_____

_____

_____

_____

4 Is there any apprehension in hearing God's voice in your prayers—theological disagreement with hearing God; fear that he may tell you to do something you don't want to do; hard to tell the difference between your own thoughts and God's prompting?

_____

_____

_____

_____

I believe God has spoken to me, clearly and about specific matters. Once I heard his voice in Colorado along side an ice-cold, clear mountain stream encrusted in ice. Another time I was driving in a car, on a two lane road, in Michigan. And, still, another time I was kneeling, under the quiet cover of early morning darkness, at the foot of my living room couch. The common thread running through the foregoing encounters with God? Prayer.

God has not "spoken" so clearly to me often, but each time he has my life changed...drastically. He, for instance, encouraged me to pursue and marry my wife, Lora. We've been married now for over 12 years. He also prompted me to be a parent, twice. I feared having children because of our financial situation, especially before our first child. He's since blessed us with greater financial freedom. In terms of starting a family, I was following the terms the world had set. God had other plans. Through prayer he let me in on those plans.

The relational encounter you have with God can change the world. Or it may just change you. If he can inspire a person who hated Christians, the Apostle Paul, to write some of the most well-known Christian writings, much of the New Testament; if he can motivate a sheep herder, Moses, to lead a na-

> God has not "spoken" so clearly to me often, but each time he has my life changed...drastically.

tion out of slavery and take them to a land that is now the setting for the end of history; if he can transform time to match his will and do infinitely more through selective relational encounters, imagine how he can transform your struggle with anger.

5 Can you think of a time or event where God let you in on his plans through your prayers? Provide details of even the slightest Divine whisper.

_____

_____

_____

_____

_____

6 What impact did it make on your life?

_____

_____

_____

_____

_____

Prayer is connecting with the Spirit of God.

Prayer is connecting with the Spirit of God. The Spirit is building a holy structure in your body. The Bible calls it a temple. God's home on Earth is in your body (1 Corinthians 3:16, 6:19; 2 Corinthians 6:16; Ephesians 2:22). It is a place where we can go, without going anywhere, to be with God. It is in prayer that we reveal our heart to God. You can praise him; worship him; ask him important questions; tell him how much you love him. He's in your heart to share eternity with you, right now! It's where you can let your requests be known, including the desire to reflect his image, as it pertains to anger.

7 God truly makes his home in you; how often do you reflect on this truth? How might the foregoing truth impact your ability to manage anger if you invested an appreciable amount of time in prayer dwelling on the fact that you are God's…well…dwelling?

_____

_____

_____

_____

_____

Heart Art

Paul says to pray on all occasions (Ephesians 6:18). Why? Because prayer…intense, focused, and continual prayer is life changing. Our lives are changed not because we somehow learn to get better at not getting angry. That is what it looks like at the surface and it is part of our effort but not the full picture. I believe that positive change occurs when we are inspired by a relational encounter that puts the purpose of our existence into focus, when we are given the opportunity to glimpse the truly important elements in our life, a values-shift occurs…including a shift in managing our anger.

> Because prayer…intense, focused, and continual prayer is life changing.

8 Can you think of a time in prayer where you were, at some level, changed by encountering God? Offer some details.

_____

_____

_____

_____

_____

Heart Keys

I believe that positive change occurs when we are inspired by a relational encounter that puts the purpose of our existence into focus….

As humans we all possess a morsel-sized nugget of God's heart and thoughts, which provide glimpses of his nature and future plans, but our view is limited. God's infinite mind, however, always includes the larger, complete picture of life. It's the bigger picture of a dramatic play that includes good and evil, prophets, kings, saints, angelic armies, an eternal city and—among an infinite number of other players... you. Prayer takes us out of the audience and beckons us to go on stage, with God and all the players in the drama.

Join me, if you will, in creating a fantastic tale to illustrate my point. You are in Stratford, England. The year is 1604. William Shakespeare sends a quick runner to find you. The purpose? To extend an invitation for you to act in one of his wildly famous plays. You arrive at the theatre with all your senses excited as you find the air dusted with the aroma of aged oak, on your tongue you can taste the myrrh-drenched mist in the near-liquid air, vivid colors of softly erect violets command full attention. You have never felt more alive yet more close to death. You step through the doors and take in the regal and the frenetically bustling view; you immediately feel both breathless and intoxicated. You somehow make your way to the front, step onto the stage area, look up, and magically start dialoguing with the most well-known and talented playwright in the history of the world.

9 If the tale above "be true," what might be going on inside of you in that moment?

_____

_____

_____

_____

_____

10 Might such an encounter have a lasting effect on you, shape some thoughts—the following day, the following week, beyond?

_____

_____

_____

_____

_____

Return to the scene. Shakespeare is speaking with animated passion and loud delight...about you and your role in his plays! He talks about his plays of antiquity, and plays yet to come. He explains his grand ideas about your role in such prodigious plays as *A Mid-Summer Night's Dream*, *Hamlet*, and *Romeo and Juliet*. As Shakespeare is focused on you and your newfound role in his historical plays, do you drift in mundane or angry thought? Are you, for example, in the back of your mind...still fuming over the milk that spilled on your new carpet, recalling how insensitive your spouse has been, still annoyed that a friend hasn't returned your calls? It isn't likely. Rather, in the encounter, haven't the previous anger-provoking issues become amusingly and insignificantly microscopic in proportion?

11 How might viewing an encounter with God, similar to your encounter with Shakespeare, affect the anger-provoking issues in your life?

_____

_____

_____

_____

_____

To this end, in light of a life-changing, values-shifting relational encounter that can be found in God through prayer, the issues triggering anger may become less significant and therefore more manageable and, perhaps, even undetectable. Meaningful encounters with God can have an affect on you which can shape your thoughts regarding anger for a day, a week and beyond.

> To this end, in light of a life-changing, values-shifting relational encounter that can be found in God through prayer, the issues triggering anger may become less significant...

_____

_____

_____

_____

Heart Surgery

12 Read Acts 9:1-6, 17-22. Describe who Paul was before encountering Jesus, include his anti-Christian attitudes/activities and relational distance from Jesus.

_____

_____

_____

_____

_____

13 Describe who Paul became, how he changed, after meeting Jesus. List some outward words, actions, and activities that likely came from the overflow of his heart.

_____

_____

_____

_____

_____

14 Read Romans 7:14-25. How does Paul describe himself?

_____

_____

_____

_____

_____

15 Does the way Paul honestly portrays himself surprise you, especially after the dramatic encounter he had with Jesus?

_____

_____

_____

_____

Taking Prayerful Steps Towards Overcoming Banned Anger

16 How do the following "verb" passages suggest ways in which we can move towards overcoming anger?
☑ Psalm 139:24...Invite God to Identify Anger

☑ 1 John 1:9...Engage in Repentance

☑ Psalm 147:3...Heal in Brokenness

☑ 2 Corinthians 3:17...Live in Freedom

God's Spirit can give us understanding into our anger, the roots of our anger, and the power to overcome banned anger. Take some time to do the following exercise.

17 Think of a recent time that your anger was strongly triggered. Notice what you were feeling as you were being triggered. Asking God to guide your understanding, reflect on your life and think back to the first time you can remember feeling the same way.
☑ What was happening at that time?

☑ How did that situation make you feel about yourself?

☑ Looking back, what do you believe was really true about you then?

☑ What does God say was and is true about you?

☑ Would believing this truth change your reaction in your more recent situation? If so, how?

18 According to 2 Timothy 1:7, what three elements has the Lord given to us? How might it relate to and help us achieve success in the steps above?

_____

_____

_____

_____

_____

19 How might we harness a spirit of power, choose to love others, and exercise the self-discipline to live a life increasingly free from banned anger?

_____

_____

_____

_____

_____

20 From what you've gained so far from this study, do you have a more lucid understanding of how you might move towards freedom and away from anger through God's Word and God's Spirit? Write a summary of your thoughts.

_____

_____

_____

_____

_____

Humor, Reflection, & Encouragement

"My mother used to say, 'He who angers you conquers you!' But my mother was a saint."

—*Elizabeth Kenny*

"Prayer is strong medicine"

—*From the CD*
Strong Medicine by Bryan Duncan

"Therefore I tell you, whatever you ask for in prayer, believe that you have received it and it will be yours."

—*Jesus, Mark 11:24*

Adrenaline Rush

Ideas to pump your heart

Spend time with God, pouring your heart out to him.

HeartMender Memory Verse

"Now the Lord is the Spirit, and where the Spirit of the Lord is, there is freedom. And we, who with unveiled faces all reflect the Lord's glory, are being transformed into his likeness with ever-increasing glory, which comes from the Lord, who is the Spirit." (2 Corinthians 3:17-18)

Closing Prayer

Lord, thank you for our time together. We pray that continuous, supernatural encounters with you might change us and make us more like you, including a meaningful change in the way we handle our anger. In the end, we do not really know how to pray because of our limited understanding. Thank you that you step in and take care of us, that you make sure that nothing is lost and all is gained for those who follow you and constantly crave your presence. Protect us from the evil one who wants to disrupt our prayer life and keep us separate from you. Thank you for gracing us with your presence! Amen!

Homework

 This week concentrate on prayer and the memory verse. Take time away to pray. Take time away from television, the internet, and even others this week. Make connecting with God through prayer your highest priority.

❷ **Do:** Week 9 in preparation for next week's group.

Bride: Living in the Heart of Redemptive Community

"Encourage one another daily...so that none of you may be hardened by sin's deceitfulness."
—Hebrews 3:13

Heart Starters

"We are like one-winged angels. It's only when we help each other that we can fly."
—Luciano de Crescenzo

"You're the only family I've got, I won't let you down."
—From the movie Top Gun

Opening Prayer

Lord, thank you for bringing us together again. Lord, this week's group is unique since we are living out this lesson in the moment, together. Help us not to merely be hearers of your Word but also doers of your Word. Your Word and your voice bring hope and life, each increases our faith, blots out our sin, and transforms our nature. Help us to encourage one another daily as your Word says—to our eternal benefit and to your glory. Let your love, grace, and truth guide us as we seek to help and encourage one another in your name. Amen.

Heartwork at Home Review

- Share with the group some details about what God has done in your life as a result of your intense, dedicated, and passionate focus on him through prayer. Include details about how you may have decreased attention on certain elements in your week in order to increase space for God.

• Discuss with your group any values-shifting themes, anger mitigation, increase in spiritual warfare, change in attitude towards daily activities, and the like.

_____

_____

_____

_____

_____

Constructing a Relational Network

Recently I watched a television special on the destructive affects of steroid use among young adult males. In the TV special two men who were taking the illegal substance were interviewed. The young men described both the benefits and the drawbacks of steroid use. To them the benefits of increased strength and enhanced athleticism outweighed the drawbacks so they continued using (a decision with which I heartily disagree).

One of the drawbacks? The drug tended to make the men more aggressive and prone to anger, often explosive anger. Each described the anger as intense and uncontrollable. In order to support one another and increase their chances of success in increased strength and athletic ability via the drug, the two made a pact to help the other control his anger. When one would become enraged the other would work to calm and redirect his anger. Since they attended the same college and worked together, they were successfully able to closely monitor the other's behavior and help manage anger when needed.

1 What parallels can you draw between the relationship the men had and relationships in the church—helping the other control anger, covenantal relationship, working together to achieve a goal?

_____

_____

_____

_____

2 Is there a similar relationship in your life where the other person has dedicated his/her energy to helping you succeed in managing your anger? Offer details to your answer.

_____

_____

_____

_____

Heart Monitor

Interestingly, the young men seemed to jump at the opportunity to help the other with his struggle. And chances are there are people who look forward to helping you with the struggles you have, including anger, because they want you to succeed in your goals, just like the athletes' desire to see the other succeed. Indeed, God has set up a communal system so that there is a pool of people that can help you in your quest to overcome anger and pursue God; and, in turn, there are also people that you are uniquely suited to help. Every part in the body serves a purpose. And our gifts are best utilized when we are building up the church (1 Corinthians 14:12).

> God has set up a communal system so that there is a pool of people that can help you in your quest to overcome anger...

3 What segment of service to the church most interests you—what brand of giving makes your heart come alive?

_____

_____

_____

_____

4 What do the following verses say about how we should interact with each other in the church?
- Acts 2:44-47

_____

_____

_____

♦ Romans 12:4-8

_____

_____

_____

♦ Hebrews 3:13

_____

_____

_____

5 What kind of help, if any, have you received from others in an attempt to help you overcome anger—helpful advice, seemingly random suggestions, spiritual direction, accountability? What has been the most helpful?

_____

_____

_____

_____

Personally I have been helped beyond measure with anger by the Church,

Personally I have been helped beyond measure with anger by the Church, a redemptive community of Christ followers. Faithful followers of Jesus that have come along side me and sacrificed for me in countless ways. They are professional therapists, mentors, teachers, and authors of books. Others are volunteer soldiers of compassion, in love with Jesus, and tireless curators of the heart. And, as I look back, I can see clearly that God put a desire in my heart, at least for a season, to travel on their path, looking for help. In many ways, I've "hitched my wagon" to some very faithful, wise, and loving people; they've become my "watchmen on the walls," and, through relationships with each, I've been blessed beyond measure.

6 Read Proverbs 12:26. What kind of people do you surround yourself with—at work, church, recreation? Describe their effect on your life, positive or negative. Discuss some of the details with the group.

_____

_____

_____

_____

Recently I had lunch with one of the "watchmen." He's a super-hero with a tender and generous heart, disguised as a small business owner. He's not perfect, obviously...what human can be this side of Paradise? But I know this one thing about him, it's something that I have experienced in fewer than a dozen relationships in my entire 40 years of life on this planet: he genuinely and continually has my best interest at heart. It's an attitude that Paul laid out in Philippians 2:3-4. And the transforming power of this type of relationship cannot be underestimated as it causes us to, like Paul put it later in the passage, "shine like stars in the universe" (2:15). Stars, like our sun, are not casually dismissed...rather they are described as brilliant, warm, welcomed each day and, in a very real sense, life sustaining. My friend, the watchman, comes close to the foregoing description.

> Recently I had lunch with one of the "watchmen"...he genuinely and continually has my best interest at heart.

7 Can you think of a person where you could say that he/she exhibited life-sustaining passions or attributes? Have you ever wished you could "hitch yourself" to that person's wagon to learn, grow, mature and, at some level, transform your anger?

_____

_____

_____

_____

_____

8 Read Matthew 16:18. What promise does Jesus give?

_____

_____

_____

_____

_____

9 How much confidence does the passage give you that you are "hitched" to the right wagon?

1   2   3   4   5   6   7   8   9   10
Very Little Confidence   A Lot of Confidence

_____

_____

_____

Heart Guard

Satan wants us to be cynical about the church and, unfortunately, he's had some devastating success. A

Satan wants us to be cynical about the church and, unfortunately, he's had some devastating success. As a result, many people are convinced that the church flat-out ignores hurting people. Yet despite what some may say, I believe God has "stacked the deck" in the Church's favor.

10 Consider 1 Timothy 3:15. According to the passage, what is the church—and what do you think the imagery and/or metaphors attempt to communicate? (vs.17)

_____

_____

_____

_____

11 Read John 6:66-68. The Twelve could have easily left with the crowd; what reason did Simon Peter give Jesus for staying—why have you stayed with the Church?

_____

_____

_____

_____

_____

_____

Heart Art

It had been over a year since Brett and Olivia, a young couple at our church, had their first child. Brett approached me one day in church; he wanted to confess some angry feelings he had over his wife's reluctance to follow his "helpful" advice. Most of Brett's advice for his wife seemed to center around nutrition and exercise. His passion and energy towards his new-found interest in her eating and exercise habits seemed just ever-so-slightly out of place.

12 What specific action did Brett take to initiate the conversation above?

_____

_____

_____

_____

13 List some elements that were likely parts of my relationship with Brett in order for me to be able to draw the conclusion: "slightly out of place."

_____

_____

_____

_____

Over several conversations, some at the gym and others in my home, I sensed that Brett was developing an even deeper resentment towards Olivia. When I suggested that he seemed to be frustrated by his wife to an ever-increasing degree, he agreed but said he wasn't sure why he was feeling the way he did. Connecting what I knew about Brett with his "slightly

Over several conversations, some at the gym and others in my home, I sensed that Brett was developing an even deeper resentment towards Olivia.

out of place" words about diet and exercise, I offered the following statement and question, "Brett, it's been a year since you had your child, might you be feeling angry because Olivia still hasn't lost the pregnancy weight?" At that Brett hung his head and began to cry. As he was crying I said, "And you fear the inability to love her well as you once did because her weight has made you feel less attracted to her." At that he put his hands over his face and sobbed bitterly.

14 How many conversations centered on this one topic before evidence of Brett's brokenness (sobbing due to fear of not loving his wife unconditionally) surfaced?

_____

_____

_____

_____

_____

Realizing he genuinely repented from his heart, she eagerly forgave him...

After some time together in prayer and more conversation Brett got up, went home, and confessed his anger and fear to his wife. She had obviously "felt" his angry pressure to change something about herself but she wasn't sure what it was...until he revealed it to her. Realizing he genuinely repented from his heart, she eagerly forgave him, and the miracle of reconciliation transformed segments of their hearts that night, priceless fragments they may carry forever for the purpose of adorning eternity.

15 What part did the "church" play in orchestrating a way of helping Brett kick some banned anger out of his life?

_____

_____

_____

_____

_____

In the time since the event Olivia hadn't had much success in losing her weight. Yet Brett seems to have been liberated to love her more now than ever. The event seemed to be a turning point in their relationship, one marked by growth and attractive maturity.

Heart Surgery

16 atch the steps from Week 8 with the corresponding excerpts of Brett's story by drawing a line connecting each.

Week 8 Steps	Excerpts of Brett's Story
Psalm 139:24...Invite God to Identify Anger	"Brett genuinely repented from the heart."
1 John 1:9...Engage in Repentance	"Brett confessed some angry feelings...."
Psalm 147:3...Heal in Brokenness	"Brett...is liberated to love her more now than ever."
2 Corinthians 3:17...Live in Freedom	"...reconciliation is transforming segments of their hearts."

17 Does it surprise you that the four prayerful steps to overcoming banned anger from last week's group so closely match with the four practical steps Brett took in overcoming his anger? Please explain your thoughts.

_____

_____

_____

_____

_____

18 Read Ephesians 2:11-22. How does the passage assure you that no matter where you are now, you are not complete...you are still under construction—might that include your anger?

_____

_____

_____

_____

_____

_____

19 Read Matthew 16:24-25. What did Jesus tell his followers to do? (Consider this: the modern day equivalent to the cross is the electric chair or a gas chamber.)

_____

_____

_____

_____

_____

Jesus wants his followers to willfully execute the sinful parts of their lives with deadly accuracy so they (we) can live a life reflective of God.

Jesus wants his followers to willfully execute the sinful parts of their lives with deadly accuracy so they (we) can live a life reflective of God. Think through this and the last two weeks' lessons. Discuss in practical terms what it might look like for you to die to anger and live for Jesus. Frame your thoughts in categories of how the following would be intimately involved in managing your anger: the church (followers of Jesus), an encounter of the Spirit through prayer, and an intense study of God's Word.

Heart Break — Charting Progress

Take a few moments to gauge where your heart is right now. Consider any thoughts, views, or major life-themes that may have changed or even slightly shifted since working through this anger management guide. Write your thoughts in the inspiration organizer below.

Who I was...	Who I have become, so far...
Before this session I thought...	After this session I think...

20 What passage, quote, group interaction, spiritual urging, do you think contributed to the change or shift? How might your interactions with God and others be different as a result of the change?

_____

_____

_____

_____

_____

Humor, Reflection, & Encouragement

"Half the time when brothers wrestle, it's just an excuse to hug each other."

—James Patterson

"A candle loses nothing by lighting another candle."

—Erin Majors

"...Friendship is precious, not only in the shade, but in the sunshine of life, and thanks to a benevolent arrangement the greater part of life is sunshine."

—*Thomas Jefferson*

Adrenaline Rush

Ideas to pump your heart

Watch for attacks from Satan at church, home, on the road, and in the workplace. Pray for God's protection and intervention.

HeartMender Memory Verse

"...encourage one another daily...so that none of you may be hardened by sin's deceitfulness." (Hebrews 3:13)

Closing Prayer

Lord, thank you for another awesome experience with you and with those who have devoted themselves to you. Who is like you, Lord? You are the creator of the universe yet you have made our anger a priority, right here...right now, and for eternity. Help us to help each other while we are here. Our time is short and our understanding is limited. We therefore need your help so that your will is done here on Earth as it is in Heaven. Help us so that we can live simply, by faith in you and by trusting the church that you set up, with the foundation of truth, and walls that cannot be torn down by Satan. You are powerful and you are good. Thank you for concerning yourself with our anger. Help us follow your path so that we can overcome the things you want us to overcome and embrace the things you want us to embrace. Thank you for gracing us with your presence! Amen!

Homework

❶ **Read:** Ephesians 2:1-22.

❷ **Pray:** for the unity of followers of Jesus.

❸ **Write:** a dramatic scene of a past or current relationship that is going through a rough or tumultuous time, where anger exists causing a rift between you and the other person. Create the scene through a redemptive framework, where you offer opportunities to reconcile using what you've learned from this guide and from personal experience. Create two endings, one where reconciliation occurs and another where the person refuses to reconcile. Create a picture of what life might be like with and without reconciliation. Describe your overall response to both endings.

❹ **Memorize:** Hebrews 3:13.

Gospel: What it Takes to Manage Anger for Life

"...he who began a good work in you will carry it on to completion until the day of Christ Jesus."

—*Philippians 1:6*

Heart Starters

"You aren't wealthy until you have something money can't buy."

—*Garth Brooks*

"...remember that...you were separate from Christ, excluded from citizenship in Israel and foreigners to the covenants of the promise, without hope and without God in the world. But now in Christ Jesus you who once were far away have been brought near through the blood of Christ."

—*Ephesians 2:12-13*

Opening Prayer

Lord, here we are for the last time in this setting, looking to you with a longing in our hearts to reflect your character. We know that we will have struggles this side of heaven. But in the middle of the storms that come in our lives and thunder around us...our hearts will be calm because of you. You give faith, hope, and love. None of these would we possess if it were not for you giving them to us with all generosity and total sacrifice. You are an awesome God who wants his creation to reflect his character. Give us the ability to love and support each other in our last time together. Amen.

Heartwork at Home Review

Share the story that you wrote in the previous week's lesson. What did you feel as you wrote the stories? Let others know what you think about their stories as well. Be open and honest. Vigorously encourage each other when the story warrants.

A Case Study of a Compelling Gospel at Work

Diane felt bitter because she felt unloved.

Diane and Jack were non-believers when they pursued counseling several decades ago. After returning from their honeymoon, frequent arguments broke out over money, issues with in-laws, and problems adjusting to sharing a small, one bedroom flat; contemptuous name-calling began and persisted. Jack felt angry because he felt disrespected. Diane felt bitter because she felt unloved. Not surprisingly, both emotional brands can be traced back to session two, "Why Can't I Just Get What I Want?", where an interference of satisfaction necessarily becomes fertile ground for growing seeds of anger, especially for those who are far from Christ.

1 Where would you say you are in your relationship with Jesus Christ?

1	2	3	4	5	6	7	8	9	10
I have no relationship with Jesus

I have a very close relationship with Jesus

_____

_____

_____

There are various levels of spiritual growth and development in our relationship with Jesus. Some people are not identified with Jesus. Others are young followers (new believers) of Jesus, discovering the elementary facets of Jesus. Others, still, are adult Christians. They are in process, facing a series of choices as they grow and mature. Finally, there are mature believers. Such believers know both triumphant victory and humiliating defeat but have not given up, they've been refined by trials.

Unidentified with Jesus: A Life Characterized by Fully Relying on Self

Jack and Diane didn't identify themselves as Christians. They were both spiritually unborn. Neither wanted or was even aware that Jesus could "bring everything [including anger] under his control…" (Philippians 3:21). They did not look to Jesus for help because Jesus was far from them. They both needed eternal salvation.

2 Read Ephesians 2:8-10. How does a person receive eternal salvation (John 3:16; Romans 3:21-26; Romans 10:9,10)? Describe in your own words the essence of a gift—what must a person do to receive a gift?

_____

_____

_____

_____

_____

If you have not received the free gift of salvation, you can do so by talking to the leader/facilitator of this group or by talking directly to Jesus. You can also go to the Appendix of this workbook. There you will find details on how you can begin an eternal relationship with Jesus.

If you have not received the free gift of salvation, you can do so by talking to the shepherd of this group or by talking directly to Jesus.

Young Believer: A Life Characterized by a Willingness to Change

After a long struggle in their marriage, Diane and Jack separated. While Diane stayed with her parents, feeling fearful and desperate for hope, her mom gave her the Bible Diane had gotten as a Christmas gift when she was a small child. Diane sat for a few moments and then prayed asking God if the Bible was an answer to her prayers. With light from a street lamp, she opened it and began reading the Bible, for the first time ever. She read the following words from the book of John:

> *"In the beginning was the Word, and the Word was with God, and the Word was God. He was with God in the beginning. Through him all things were made; without him nothing was made that has been made. In him was life, and that life was the light of men. The light shines in the darkness, but the darkness has not understood it"* (1-4).

In an instant the fear she experienced was gone. Interestingly, she felt both emotionally calm and spiritually convicted. She sensed God was speaking to her. She continued reading:

"He was in the world...Yet to those who received him, to those who believed in his name, he gave the right to become children of God..." (10-12).

She could barely finish the last phrase when she began to weep and pray. Diane prayed for forgiveness of her sins. She prayed, as the passage had stated, to receive Jesus, along with other personal and private prayers. She now identified herself as a Christian, a new believer. She was aware that Jesus had transformed her life.

3 What transformation occurred in Diane when she pursued God by praying and reading the Bible? How did she identify herself and what was she aware of at the end?

_____

_____

_____

_____

_____

4 James 4:8 states that if we come near to God, he will come near to us. Such was true for Diane. Can you think of a time when you pursued God and, in doing so, experienced a greater relational closeness with him? Share some thoughts with your group.

_____

_____

_____

_____

_____

About that time Jack came to see Diane. He wanted to tell her about the dream he had that night. He explained that his dream consisted of Diane receiving a Bible as a small child. Before he could utter another word Diane burst into tears. Diane then reached over, picked up the Bible and held it out so that Jack could see it. At that, Jack began to cry tears of joy and praise. It was the Bible he had pictured in his dream.

In the same night, but in a different manner, Jack had pursued God and, it appeared, he spoke to Jack through a transformational dream. Jack identified himself as a believer, reconciled with Diane and they went home to start their new lives, together.

Adult Believers: A Life Characterized by a Continuous Crossroad of Choices

Over the course of the next 30 years Diane and Jack raised five children; they had two heartbreaking miscarriages. The oldest son was killed in war. The other son was one of the most decorated men in his battalion. He is happily married and living on the East coast. The oldest daughter married an airline pilot and is living happily with two children in the Southwest. The second oldest daughter decided to stay single and started a highly successful charitable organization. Their youngest daughter struggled with homosexual desires and eventually died in a tragic car accident. Jack and Diane had good and hard times while struggling with life and anger. At times they handled anger well and other times they did not.

> Jack and Diane had good and hard times while struggling with life and anger.

5 If Jack and Diane were a couple in this support group, what sort of counsel would you offer in order to love and encourage them as fellow spiritual sojourners who have struggled in profound ways, including an ongoing struggle with anger?

_____

_____

_____

_____

Mature Believers: A Life Characterized by a Near-Total Transformation of the Heart

Jack and Diane pursued a supernatural course; they pursued the Gospel. In the Gospel of Jesus Christ, both found power, and that power transformed their lives, including their struggles with anger. Others experienced the transformation second-hand, and were blessed by it. People gravitated towards Jack's positive and hopeful outlook while others felt loved and encouraged by Diane as her spiritually effervescent passion for Jesus bubbled over onto their lives. As in all relationships however there were still difficult moments. But following moments of banned anger with others, both Jack and Diane sought to reconcile by repenting of sin while humbly seeking forgiveness from those they had hurt with anger.

Heart Keys

To Jack and Diane, the Gospel was compelling because its power transformed their lives, including their struggles with anger.

To Jack and Diane, the Gospel was compelling because its power was transforming their lives, including their struggles with anger. Each were becoming, as James put it, Christians who were "mature and complete" (1:4).

6 Discuss the following statement in your group. The more Diane's and Jack's relationship with Jesus grew (where each increasingly lived a Gospel lifestyle), the more they were able to, with increasing ease, effectively and attractively manage their anger.

_____

_____

_____

_____

_____

Living a Gospel Lifestyle to Manage Anger for a Lifetime

There are four areas, along with the lessons from the last few weeks that can help you to grow in your faith, mature as a Christian, and break free from the bonds of anger through a biblically-based, Gospel-rich lifestyle: *Brokenness; Repentance; Gratitude; and Dying to self, Living for Jesus.*

Lifestyle of Brokenness: Honestly Looking at How We Hurt Others with Our Anger

Many years ago, during a difficult stretch in Jack's life, Jack frequently lashed out in anger at Diane. One time in particular she didn't return the fire as she had so often done in the past. Instead she spoke to him with pure kindness. Her steady and reasoned voice seemed like a test to him so, looking for a fight, he escalated his attack, using harsh and demeaning terms designed to harm and shame. But the kind words offered by Diane only increased in intensity, and with redemptive honesty. Leaning forward she said, "I know that you love me. I wonder what it would look like for you to honestly face how your anger has worked to crush the spirit of the one you love?"

7 Read Psalm 51:16-17. It's a passage that David wrote after he honestly looked at how he had hurt God and others. According to the passage, what did God want from David?

_____

_____

_____

_____

_____

8 Psalm 147:3 states that God heals the brokenhearted and binds up their wounds. What do you think about the passage—how does it make you feel?

_____

_____

_____

_____

_____

Later in the day, with a broken spirit, Jack apologized for and repented of his anger. He and Diane wept together and held each other. Jack experienced brokenness and a transformational, godly sorrow, a significant turning point in their lives.

In 2 Corinthians 7:9-10, Paul states that godly sorrow over a harm done brings about repentance. Repentance is the key to immediate change and can be life-transforming when lived out on a daily basis.

Lifestyle of Repentance: Deciding to Turn Away From Anger

To repent literally means to "turn away from."

To repent literally means to "turn away from." According to Romans 2:4, it is the kindness of God that leads us to repentance. Mark 1:15 states that we have the ability to believe the gospel only after we repent. Acts 20:21 states that turning to God in repentance is necessary for faith. Repentance, it turns out, is not only the key to eternal salvation but also necessary for transformation in our character and growth after we become Christians, including a transformation in our attitudes towards anger.

9 What do the following verses tell us about the desirable, life-altering changes—our ability to believe the gospel, prompting angels to party, behavioral shifts, relational restoration—that accompany repentance?

◆ Luke 15:10

_____

_____

◆ Luke 15:21-24

_____

_____

◆ Luke 17:3-4

_____

_____

_____

10 When Jack broke free from the bonds of banned anger he assumed the role of servant-leader to his wife. What would repentance look like for you? Share encouraging responses with your support group.

_____

_____

_____

_____

_____

According to Luke 15:21-24, the son repented of his sin causing the broken relationship between he and his Father to be restored. The Father's response? A wild celebration to express gratitude.

Lifestyle of Gratitude: Trading an Angry Heart for a Heart of Worship

Diane's father, a wealthy man, once gave a $1,000.00 gift card to Diane and one to her sister, Dawn, for Christmas. But the gift made Dawn angry because she believed that her dad had the means to offer far more. She immediately phoned a friend to angrily gossip about her dad's "stinginess." Diane however overflowed with a thankful heart because of her father's generosity. She danced around her house, praising and worshipping God. She then phoned her father to thank him.

11 Who do you think experienced more freedom, Diane or Dawn? Why? Given the circumstances, what do you think your response might have been to the gift card?

_____

_____

_____

_____

Christ has set us free. According to Galatians 5:1, freedom is central to the life of a believer. The longer a person is a Christian the more freedom he/she should experience, regardless of circumstances. A truly free Christian will be content no matter what. Paul calls it a secret (Philippians 4:12). It's something that mature believers understand. When Paul penned those words he was old, cold, and laying on a dirt prison floor, recovering from recent beatings. He was a mature Christian, free in spirit, and filled with gratitude.

Christ has set us free. According to Galatians 5:1, freedom is central to the life of a believer.

12 Read Acts 16:22-25. How did Paul and Silas respond to the mistreatment and beatings, with anger or worship? How would you have responded?

_____

_____

_____

Cultivating a heart of gratitude can increase your success in managing your anger while, at the same time, lead to a lifestyle marked by a deeper level of worship by deciding, on a daily basis, to replace the old life (death) with a new one (life).

> "Don't worry about anything; instead, pray about everything. Tell God what you need, and thank him for all he has done."
>
> Philippians 4:6, NLT

Lifestyle of Dying to Self, Living for Jesus: Replacing an Old Life with a New Life

As Jack and Diane grew in their relationship with Jesus, anger subsided as they began a process of "dying" to self and living for Jesus. In the slow process of healing and change they began to trust God, to ever-increasing degrees, with the things that mattered to them the most. At times it felt like death, and it was (death of the sinful self), but it ignited fresh life...the full and abundant life that Jesus talked about in the Gospels.

13 According to the following verses, where and how is life found, and how is it described?

+ John 1:4

_____

_____

+ John 10:10

_____

_____

+ Philippians 1:21

_____

_____

14 Read Philippians 3:12-21. Might the term "everything" in verse 21 include your anger? What might your life look like if Christ brought your anger under his control?

_____

_____

_____

_____

15 What are we to rid ourselves of? (vs.8) Name some "old self" practices (vs.9) that you have not yet taken off. List some "new self" behaviors (vs.10) that you have already put on.

_____

_____

_____

_____

16 Read Ephesians 4:22-32; 5:1-2. According to the passages, what might happen to our anger if we were to imitate God, live a life of love, give ourselves up for Jesus (like he did for us), and make ourselves (our old-self anger) a fragrant sacrifice to God?

_____

_____

_____

_____

Well Done Good and Faithful Servant

My friend Jack died in 1995. He is no longer being transformed daily but is now complete and fully alive through Christ, in heaven—greatly missed by all, including Diane. Now in her mid-80s, Diane is still in the process of transfor-

> Now in her mid-80s, Diane is still in the process of transformation, more willing than ever to gain God's reflective qualities...

mation, more willing than ever to gain God's reflective qualities, including the quality of holy, banner anger. Diane still gets angry at times but it's anger that develops slowly, it's rare and is usually displayed for good purposes, just like Paul directed.

> Transforming your anger is possible but it will require your very life...the old, sinful self.

Transforming your anger is possible but it will require your very life...the old, sinful self. But the transformation will be more than worth the price. A new life, such as Jack and Diane were pursuing, will begin to emerge, grow, and strengthen, reflecting the image of God through the power of the Gospel...the power to redeem the heart of Cain.

Humor, Reflection, & Encouragement

"If you were waiting for the opportune moment...that was it."

—Captain Jack Sparrow, Pirates of the Caribbean

"Now is the hour come.... Foes and fires are before you, and your homes far behind. Yet, though you fight upon an alien field, the glory that you reap there shall be your own forever. Oaths ye have taken: now fulfill them all..."

—J.R.R. Tolkien

"The God of peace will soon crush Satan under your feet. The grace of our Lord Jesus be with you."

—Romans 16:20

Adrenaline Rush

Ideas to pump your heart

Secretly give a gracious gift to someone who tends to stir your anger.

"A gift given in secret soothes anger." Proverbs 21:14

HeartMender Memory Verse

"May God himself, the God of peace, sanctify you through and through. May your whole spirit, soul and body be kept blameless at the coming of our Lord Jesus Christ. The one who calls you is faithful and he will do it." (1 Thessalonians 5:23-24)

Closing Prayer

Lord, thank you for meeting us in a powerful and life-altering manner in our last week together. We understand that there is a season for everything and this season is ending. But, Lord, through you we understand that you are not done. You tell us in your Word that you began a good work in us and you will complete it. Lord, give us the courage we need to walk the line of pursuing good banner anger while working to prevent harmful banned anger. Help us to repent when we are angry. Help us to pursue the resources of your Word, your Spirit, and your people that you have generously provided. Help us to die to ourselves and live for you. And help to cultivate a heart of gratitude in order to experience the full freedom that you provide. Help us to draw close to you, to overcome our struggle with anger and to glorify your name. Thank you for gracing us with your presence! Amen!

Supernatural Conviction: Poet's Heartache

"And He answered him, 'Pursue, for you shall surely overtake them and without fail recover all.'"
—*1 Samuel 30:8 (NKJV)*

"The future belongs to those who believe in the beauty of their dreams."
—*Eleanor Roosevelt*

"Success is not final, failure is not fatal: it is the courage to continue that counts."
—*Winston Churchill*

"Art is never finished, only abandoned."
—*Leonardo da Vinci*

The Heart of the Matter

"Above all else, guard your heart,
*   for it is the wellspring of life."*
—*Proverbs 4:23*

A woman recently shared a story about her struggles since getting "cured" by her well-meaning psychotherapist. She confessed that since her intensive counseling sessions with her therapist, she didn't experience outward anger like she used to but she didn't feel much passion for life anymore, either. Her complaint isn't that uncommon.

There is a temptation in counseling for the therapist to "throw out the baby with the bath water," so to speak. We sometimes want so much to "fix" the people looking for help that we crank up their time-piece gears so tight the pendulum swings to the other side and, with great force, often knocks the clock to the ground. The person ends up being "cured" but in a strange position, possessing a little less sin, but at the same time, a little less life.

There is a temptation in counseling for the therapist to "throw out the baby with the bath water," so to speak.

Ecclesiastes 7:18 states that "the man who fears God will avoid all extremes." Yet we often go to extremes when it comes to our emotions, hoping simply to vanquish an element of our lives and replace it with completely opposite feelings. "The Psalms help us understand that *every emotion is a theological statement*" (Allender/Longman, 34). When we work to rid ourselves of our emotions rather than look to our emotions to tell us something about the nature of God we are losing ground in our effort to know him better. Some of our anger is rooted in God, some anger comes from the influences of the world, and some from ourselves. We would do well not to pull out all the roots. It's the dilemma of any good gardener.

Anger's purpose in our hearts

Anger that has its roots in injustice brings us closer to what Paul wrote when he supplied us with the directive that we "be angry." We should be angry when an injustice occurs, just as God is. We should feel and express banner anger when a child is hurt by a bully, when an incoherent drunk driver smashes his car into a minivan killing a young family returning from soccer practice, or when a woman who wants to give her eight-month-old, unborn baby up for adoption following the child's birth is instead counseled by a coworker to choose abortion.

I submit that anger towards the foregoing unjust acts is an emotion that, more often than not, reflects the character of God. God's anger is righteous. Always. Our anger is rarely righteous and should be up for continual review. Always. How we as humans manage our anger may be far different than what God would do with his anger. The righteous anger that Paul talked about, the anger that Jesus and God and the Holy Spirit engaged in was and is a righteous anger. And we can peer into the Bible to get a look at the side of God's character that displays anger. God was angry at his early creation for deserting him, at Israel for infidelity, and at those who opposed Israel. He's angry at Satan, at those who follow Satan, and he was even angry at his Son, for a moment in time, when Jesus became a curse, covered in sin on the cross.

To demonstrate his anger, God used wrath (i.e., destruction) to display his intentions and emotions towards his creation. Feeling uncomfortable with God's destructive side is not helpful for those who are trying to live lives reflecting his image. Facing the full character of God is courageous as well as helpful in learning more about the character of God. In

> Anger that has its roots in injustice brings us closer to what Paul wrote when he supplied us with the directive that we "be angry."

part we learn through God's anger that he is utterly, totally, and supremely just and infinitely merciful. He is justified in and capable of destroying everything that he has made and starting over, but he instead pours out his grace and chooses to make new everything that has turned against him.

In similar manner, feeling uncomfortable with your own anger or living in denial is not helpful to managing the anger that may be just beneath the surface of many relational interactions that you may encounter. However, facing the emotional and spiritual magnitude of who we are on the inside is courageous and helpful in learning how to greater manage our anger, since God's just and merciful character and anger are reflected in those who bear his image. His image bearers reflect righteous anger due to injustice. Unfortunately, however, we also possess unrighteous anger when an injustice occurs.

To this end, as we gain a greater understanding of God's just nature, the triggers of our own anger will continually become more lucid to ever-increasing degrees of clarity. And, moreover, in the context of a transforming relationship with Jesus, the understanding, knowledge, and wisdom of how to handle or manage our anger will become much more than a mere habit that is learned. Rather, it will become a mindset that is in the process of transformation…a way of living that solves nearly every problem that each and every human who craves positive change needs: supernatural conviction.

Supernatural conviction of the heart

Supernatural conviction transcends all other elements and circumstances in life. It requires 100% participation by you and 100% participation by God. Nothing more and nothing less. Its raw truth whispers louder than the shouts of ever-changing feelings that often cause our hearts to wander and rage.

Supernatural conviction boasts a surround sound like voice that beckons us to rush into the relational, spiritual, and the physical unknown of danger and risk…even though our natural convictions tell us to abandon all pursuit. It is not unlike a fireman who rushes into a burning house ablaze with red-hot fire that will at any moment collapse in on itself…and all for a higher purpose than his own life, the fireman still moves to preserve, save, and

Supernatural conviction transcends all other elements and circumstances in life.

protect. The fireman may lose his life, but nothing in his heart was compromised; he lived out his calling. His heart was guarded to the point where he could live out his conviction to die. For this reason, we can say he truly lived. His death casts bright stage lights on his conviction. And, for good or for ill, our eventual deaths will cast similar lights on our convictions.

Living in the Heart of God

Living our lives with supernatural conviction offers us a snap shot of our world where all the lesser images are cropped, merely leaving space for the one or two elements that truly matter in life. The hyper-valuable images are then projected on a panoramic screen so large, so completely encompassing, and wildly captivating that nothing else is in view...time's forgotten, gold streets are forged, gates of entry number 12, and a river of colorful redemption runs from the throne of the Almighty. God smiles and a life, your intensely valuable life—that is still filled with trials on this side of heaven, has...through Jesus, overcome the world. You then laugh with the thunderous howl of angels and wonder why anger ever had such a tight grip on your life.

> This is where we meet God and experience his transforming love and grace. On his generous terms.

This is where we meet God and experience his transforming love and grace. On his generous terms. In the place and time of his choosing. It's where he offers you the opportunity to find freedom, liberty, and strength to redeem the heart of Cain, forging it into the heart of a poet, filled with utterances from the Spirit, and overflowing with words resembling choice fruit and indescribably attractive and pure aromas.

Read on, study, ponder, wait, pursue, invite, and live. An all-star cast of Saints have gone through the same things you're going through, many struggle alongside you now and others will fight on to victory after you've gone. This is your time to be more than your anger. This is your time to define yourself not as an angry man or an angry woman, but rather as a redeemed image bearer who is angry only rarely and slowly for the purpose of destroying evil and redeeming others so that they may accept the invitation to taste and see that the Lord is good and powerful. You are on God's side and you are winning. *Press on!*

Salvation Prayer

Are you at Peace with God?

Try as we may, if we have anything in our conscience that is contrary to God, we will not be able to experience true peace in our hearts.

We need to have peace with God before we can experience true, lasting peace that conquers anger. Each of us has a God-shaped vacuum—we were created to experience a relationship with him. The only way this relationship with our heavenly Father can occur is through his son, Jesus Christ (John 14:6 "I am the way, the truth and the life. No one comes to the Father except through me").

We need to have peace with God before we can experience true, lasting peace that conquers anger.

So, first and foremost, consider if you are absolutely certain that you have a relationship with God through Jesus Christ. If you have any doubt that you have accepted what Jesus did on the cross personally for your sins, and if you're not one hundred percent sure if you have received his free gift of eternal life, this is where to start to experience true peace. If you will but pray a simple prayer like this and mean it in your heart, God has promised to save you.

> *Dear Lord, I acknowledge that I have not followed your way. I ask now for you to forgive me of all my sin. I believe that you willingly died on the cross for my sins, rose again, and reign as my Savior; thank you that I am now pure in your sight because of what Jesus did on the cross for me. You love me like no other, and desire to come into my life. I accept your gift of salvation. Guide me, Lord, and grant me peace. Thank you. In Jesus' name. Amen.*

If you just prayed this prayer of salvation for the first time, all of heaven is rejoicing! God has saved you from your sin; he loves you and is with you! He has come into your life and will never leave you (Hebrews 13:5). This is the most crucial decision you can make because not only will your new relationship with Christ influence your life on earth, but it will also assure you of eternal life (1 John 5:12). Christianity is not about religion; it's a growing relationship with the living God who longs to fellowship with us.

As a believer in Christ, you can deepen your relationship with him through:

- Prayer (Psalm 50:15; Matthew 6:5-13; 1 Thessalonians 5:17)

- Praise and worship (Psalm 50:23; James 4:8)

- Bible study (Psalm 119:11; 2 Timothy 3:15-17)

- Serving others (Matthew 25:34-46)

- Spending time with other believers (Hebrews 10:25)

You may not be ready to take this step to pray the prayer. It's not about just saying the words with your mouth, it's the faith that matters. Take time if you need to search your heart and soul. Ask questions. Ponder the answers. Seek God for understanding. Christ is knocking at your heart, but you're the only one who can decide if you want to open the door to let him in. "Yet to all who received him, to those who believed in his name, he gave the right to become children of God" (John 1:12).

> Christ is knocking at your heart, but you're the only one who can decide if you want to open the door to let him in.

References

Allender, Dan B., and Tremper Longman III. *The Cry of The Soul*. Colorado Springs, CO: NavPress, 1994.

Carter, Les, and Frank Minirth. *The Anger Workbook*. Nashville, TN: Thomas Nelson, 1993.

Chapman, Gary. *Understanding and Processing Anger* audio tape. 2004.

New King James Version: The Holy Bible. Thomas Nelson, Inc.: 1982.

Childre, Doc, and Howard Martin. *HeartMath Solution:* www.heartquotes.net.

Eldredge, John. *Wild at Heart: Discovering the Secret of a Man's Soul*. Nashville, TN: Thomas Nelson, 2001.

New American Standard Bible, The Holy Bible. The Lockman Foundation: 1960.

New Living Translation, The Holy Bible. Tyndale House Publishers: 1996.

Sebranek, Patrick, Daven Kemper, and Verne Meyer. *Writers, Inc.: A Student Handbook for Writing and Learning*. Wilmington, MA: Great Source Education Group, 2001.

Stanley, Charles. *On Holy Ground: A Daily Devotional*. Nashville, TN: Thomas Nelson, 1999.

Printed in the United States
213201BV00002B/2/P

9 780977 980000